CONTENTS

INTRODUCTION TO THE WORKBOOK

This is a workbook with suggested rituals and exercises for working with the main phases of the Moon for the second half of 2017. In between these page you'll find rituals, magic spells, suggested exercises for each phase. There are astrological overviews, Tarot spreads, recipes, self-development work, and spell and ritual tool suggestions. This meant to serve as one tool in your toolkit for self-empowerment. This is meant to be paired with your own journey, your own personal work.

These writings and suggestions come from decades-long interaction with various spiritual pursuits, practices and studies. My personal concentration over the past five years has been working with the different phases of the Moon, and that is what this workbook focuses on. I have had wonderful results by doing the work, and encourage you try with an open mind. I have found it is a very natural state to live in. It is one our ancestors have lived in. It follows nature. It can be a useful tool at any stage of our own spiritual growth or awareness we find ourselves in.

It is important for me to mention that my metaphysical focus and expertise is in Tarot, not astrology. Throughout this book I sprinkle in Tarot card references to be used as references and archetypes to utilize. I believe that working with the ideas of different archetypes—whether cultural, historical, or metaphysical— can be very useful when pondering our own earthly challenges. I'm interested more in the ideas and suggestions of various spiritual, metaphysical, self-help, healing and psychological theories as well as archetypes to spark inspiration and personal resonance—not using one discipline or lens as a be-all, end-all blanket solution for everyone.

In my own personal experience, magic and self-development and self-inquiry go hand in hand. This book includes both. Magickal exercises and rituals are suggested, as well as questioning, getting clear, getting consistent with our basic wants. Hopefully this will help you as it has helped me.

Self-help work and spiritual practices are complicated, personal, and require commitment and discipline. When we do inner work, our outer world shifts, and vice versa. Like whispered spells and empty wishes, this workbook will not work if you do not. If there is no trying, no outward energy moved, no shift in mindset, belief, or self-talk, then things stay the same. However, I have found from personal experience that it takes very little time to notice change, to trust your own intuition and outside messages, and to create a different reality. Remember, what we do in the present moment will change the course of our lives in the future. This is why the present is so powerful. While you are working on things, I encourage you to listen. To pay attention to messages. To deepen into your own voice, your own messages, your own knowing. To take notes, via paper and pen. To keep track of your own life, take responsibility for such. I would also encourage you to commit to folding into a key spiritual practice and pursuit during this time. Maybe it is Reiki, Tarot, herbal medicine and healing. Maybe it is breath work or meditation, palm reading or astrology. Free writing or painting. Stretching, running, singing, or chanting. To also delve into a mind-altering practice that will support some of the exercises and suggestions in this book. To not believe everything that you think. That there is more out there, more than we can see, more than we've been shown by the dominant paradigm. That you are so capable! So special, so loved. So very worthwhile.

The end goal of doing spiritual and self-improvement work is to ultimately help others. To help the planet, our earth, our water, our air, our sky. The creatures and the other living things that communicate to us by their existence. When a bird flies right in front of us, dropping its feather. When that hibiscus petal seems to bend just to us, and us alone. To heal deep pain and damages our ancestors have unknowingly placed upon us, in the hopes that our wounding to others around us is minimal. Becoming so financially self-sufficient that we can give those who need money our own with joy and ease. So we can eventually create foundations and organizations of love and kindness, betterment and aid. To support and help the environment that has been damaged by greed and ignorance. To become, with our own behaviors, speech, and actions, examples and support to those around us. This is our responsibility as witches, as dreamers, as artists, as healers, as creators, as conscious human beings on this globe.

If something does not resonate with you in this book, do not use it. These rituals and spell work are merely suggestions and guides, different ways to spark thought and change. If a different certain spell or ritual is calling to you at a particular time, then be all means, please do that! This is your own very personal practice and only you know what is best: listen to yourself. If something rubs you the wrong way, I encourage you to do your own research! Take what you would like and leave the rest.

You do not have to believe in Wicca, neo-Paganism, self-help, hypnotism, therapy, AA, Judiasm, Catholiscim, Christianity, Zen-Buddhism, Buddhism, any organized religion, in Astrology, or even anything higher than you to utilize these exercises. (Though all of the suggested exercises take from all of the above-mentioned viewpoints.) There should however, be an openness to energy work, mindfulness practice, and a curiosity to learn more in a specific spiritual/self-development zone that interests your inner voice. You *do* have to believe in yourself—and in your incredible power and potential. I invite you to reconsider your power, your beauty, your impact.

It would be very encouraged to look into your own specific background and their spiritual practices. Ancestors, traditions, philosophies. Every culture has one; there might be several from your own background you resonate with. Do your own research and your own work in this realm. Again, this takes time. We've all been raised in a capitalist, hetereonormative, patriarchial culture. I urge you to examine why you are doing this— why you buy what you buy, what you sell, and why. I encourage everyone to connect first and foremost to their background when working their spiritual practice: not take, steal, or profit from another's. Don't mindlessly grab at images, thoughts, deities. Think about what kinds of entitlement your privilege or lack of privilege does or does not give you access to. I encourage you to take the time to develop your own view, voice, and content—not just repost, grab and regurgatite from other sources—including this one!

No matter where you are, no matter who you are reading this, I have love for you, I want the best or better for you. I hope you possess and practice love, forgiveness, and kindness with yourself to create your own most beloved reality for you and your loved ones, for those who have served you, and those who have done you wrong. May all of us create a more positive, kinder, more loving, more creative world. May you be healthy and safe. Bless you and blessed be!

WHY THE MOON

Because she's a celestial anchor. Because she's both tethered and free. Because she's complicated. Because we can feel her inside of us. When she's inside of one of us, she's inside of us all. Because she's tied to the tides. Because the earliest people obeyed her orbit, timed their months and holidays and celebrations and agriculture to her, and part of that lineage is still in us, cell phone light be damned.

Because she's both the lullaby rocking the baby to sleep and the electrons of wired loops keeping grown-ups pacing up and down in hallways, all through the night. Because she's heard ambulance sirens, because she's seen every crazy battle from spears to assault rifles, every buffalo herd race over the grasslands. Because we came from the salt water, millions and millions of years ago, and that salt water is still inside of us.

Because she's the divine feminine, every single part and sigh and whisper and scream and giggle, each tiny girl's toes, each teenager's first coat of nail polish, each grandmother's favorite recipe. The different slivers are reflection of our most anguished state, our calmest Mona Lisa smiles. You are lit up with her; she lights the cells within, her fading lumina allows you the space to turn inside and fade. She's complicated and changing, familiar and distant all at once.

Because she wants you to gather, wants you to revel, wants you to celebrate, to harvest and solace one another. The messenger of tears, the bringer of truths. A rock and a optic illusion lightbulb and a muse and a prayer and a song and and a scream or a stifle and a scourge and a spiral of time. La Luna lights up the night, our subconscious, where the deep mind lives. The hands of our internal clocks rotate around her luminescent center.

Because she's back. That bitch, that witch, she's back. Because for some of us she's the best friend and for some the worst enemy. Universal sisterhood sounds so sweet but it is really hard. It might be another chore, a job, an emotional labor—on top of all the rest. She's here to remind us that everything sacred comes back around again. And right now we are ready to dismantle the patriarchy: but we must do so together. With our mindset, our thought forms, our actions and our outreach we are bringing forth a new form of soft power and sisterhood, for all women, weirdos, femmes, non-binary humans—anyone who has felt othered, punished, or abused for being who they simply are.

Tracking time and worshipping by the light of the Moon has been noted across the globe. The Moon was human beings' original calendar. The earliest civilizations relied on the light of the Moon in the desert as a way to mark the passing of time. Without seasons in this climate, the Moon made an easy timekeeper. Hundreds of years later, humans relied on the various phases of the Moon for agricultural purposes; to this day there are agricultural calendars that let farmers and gardeners know when it is time to plant seeds, trim, harvest and till. Biodynamics have shown that the Earth is more fertile during Full Moons.

People who bleed often are synced up to the Moon. Not every woman bleeds and not everyone who bleeds is a woman. An average person's cycle is about 28 days long—obviously around the same cycle as one lunar phase. If you bleed, you can track your cycle to the Moon's. There is much more research and books you can read on this topic. There was a the shift from the reverence for the matriarchy and divine feminine to the misogyny associated with PMS and bleeding. If you are a person who bleeds getting in touch with your cycles and how your body, mind, and spirit act during each phase is a wonderful way to deepen intuition and connect more dots in your self-care map.

The Triple Goddess and the personal Trinity

A common symbol in the occult and in Paganism is that of the "Triple Goddess", or the one of the primary deities worshipped. The symbol is of a waxing crescent, full, and waning crescent moon. These three different states are meant to symbolize different aspects of divine femininity: the maiden, the mother, and the crone. We have to note that traditionally these three aspects, coined by a man, rely on a woman's ability to give birth. Obviously we know this is bullshit, that our inherent worth has nothing to do with our child-bearing ability, i.e., our age. What I do find helpful about this symbology are the emphasis on different phases. You can be 88 years old and in a maiden phase. You could be 16 and feeling like a crone with some issue or process. We could move from crone to maiden to mother to crone and back in again in a week, around an issue. We all move, we are ever changing.

This symbol occurs cross-culturally in deities such as Isis, Hathor, and the High Priestess card from the Major Arcana. Upside down, it also resembles a womb. 3 is a very magic number: that of motion, manifestation, movement. A triangle, a witch's hat, a pointing of energy, a stool.

Other triple symbologies pop up in echoes. The three fates. The three of cups in the Tarot. The three furies. Our third eyes. It further extends the notions of oneness, otherness, thirdness. The third as a potent symbol represents going beyond the binary. It suggests the recentering, or at the very least, the inclusion of the other. There's the promise of more.

There is another important holy trinity: that of the mind/body/spirit. Facilitating any change requires full integration of the mind, the body, the spirit. Focus on one or all of these at a time. They all feed into one another. Manifestation begins in your mind, with your thoughts and mindset. The famous quote from Gandhi encapsulates this:

"Your beliefs become your thoughts, Your thoughts become your words,
Your words become your actions, Your actions become your habits,
Your habits become your values, Your values become your destiny."

Thoughts become things. We must question our core beliefs about who we think we are. Do you truly believe you are worthy, deserving, lovable, loving? If on some level you do not believe you deserve what you are working magic for then your magic will not be as successful as possible. Before you speak, respond, react, take a second to pause and question. Think about what is driving your reaction. Question your core beliefs frequently.

Our body acts out our wishes. Our body holds so much information. Trauma and habitual emotions are stored in the body. Bodies must be cared for, loved, nourished, and treated kindly. Lots of healing can take place through caring for our bodies. For those of us who carry stigma against our bodies it can be harder to work through that. Your body deserves love, care, and adoration no matter what.

Spirit helps us. Spirit gives messages, allows pathways to clear, grants us grace. Spirit can be your religion, your faith, your ancestors, messengers, angels, belief systems, the cosmos, spirit guides, ascended masters, and your intuition.

Working with these different elements, listening to them, improving and deepening our relationship to them ensures that respect for ourselves and one another will grow.

The Various Phases of the Moon

The Moon revolves counter-clockwise around the Earth. One cycle, from New Moon to New Moon takes 29.5 days to complete. While the earliest cultures operated around a Lunar Calendar, the Gregorian Calendar does not. The "Moonth" and the month are not in sync. For much of 2017, the Full Moon is in the beginning of our month, somewhere between the 9th and 12th.

There are eight full phases of the moon that Western science recognizes: New Moon, New Crescent/Waxing Crescent, First Quarter, Waxing Gibbous, Full Moon, Waning Gibbous, Last Quarter, Waning/Balsamic. The moon goes around the Earth once and spins on its axis once, all in the same amount of time, and it shows us just one face the whole time. When we look up at the Moon, what we are viewing is a scenario put into place by the Sun, the Earth, and the Moon's orbits and rotations. The earth rotates around the Sun, and the Moon around the Earth. As the Moon rotates, the rays of the Sun hit it at different angles, affecting what we see of the moon. You're actually seeing the reflected light from the Sun, bouncing off the Moon, which acts like a mirror.

The Moon is not round (or spherical). Instead, it's shaped like an egg. If you go outside and look up at the Moon, one of the small ends is pointing right at you. In this book I write about how many cultures believe Earth's origin stories to be that of the "cosmic egg."

Tides on Earth are caused mostly by the Moon (the Sun has a smaller effect). The Moon's gravity pulls on Earth's oceans. High tide aligns with the Moon as Earth spins underneath. Another high tide occurs on the opposite side of the planet because gravity pulls Earth toward the Moon more than it pulls the water. Humans are mostly water. Our insides might just move around, shift, be heightened, much like the water ebbing and flowing, magnetized by the Moon's gravity.

As the Moon moves eastward away from the Sun in the sky, we see a bit more of the sunlit side of the Moon each night. A few days after the New Moon, we see a thin crescent in the western evening sky. The crescent Moon waxes, and when half of the Moon's disc is illuminated, we call it the first quarter moon. (The Moon is now one-quarter of the way through the lunar month.) From Earth, we are now looking at the sunlit side of the Moon from off to the side.The Moon continues to wax. Once more than half of the disc is illuminated, it has a shape we call gibbous. The gibbous moon appears to grow fatter each night until we see the full sunlit face of the Moon. We call this phase the Full Moon. It rises almost exactly as the Sun sets and sets just as the Sun rises the next day. The Moon has now completed one half of the lunar month.

During the second half of the lunar month, the Moon grows thinner each night, in its Waning state. Its shape is still gibbous at this point, but grows a little thinner each night. As it reaches the three-quarter point in its month, the Moon once again shows us one side of its disc illuminated and the other side in darkness— the Third Quarter or Last Quarter waning moon. However, the side that we saw dark at the First Quarter phase is now the lit side. As it completes its path the Moon is a Waning Crescent, then becomes dark, before the New Moon again.

In this book, we will be working with five phases: New, Waxing, Full, Waning, and Dark. The Moon cycle is perfectly suited to magic as it aligns with basic metaphysical and practical principles of magick and manifestation. During the New Moon we set intentions, during the Waxing cycle we take practical steps to move forward, during the Full Moon we celebrate, affirm, aim even higher, during the Waning Moon we release, work through blocks, and get rid of that which is no longer serving us. The Dark Moon is a time for finality, banishing, and deeper magic practices. I guarantee if you begin working a cycle through you will see change very quickly. By addressing the mind/body/spirit shifts will begin to take hold.

New Moon

In astronomy, New Moon is the first phase of the Moon, when it orbits as seen from the Earth, the moment when the Moon and the Sun have the same eliptical longitude. During this phase the Moon is farthest away from us viewers on Earth. We actually can't even see the moon when it is technically "new". It is a void, invisible, a blank slate. Some witches believe the New Moon to be when the moon appears completely dark. I like to work with New Moon energies on the day when the tiniest sliver of a light smile appears. The glimmering hint of possibilities is shown to us, igniting hope and imparting new beginnings. For many ancient cultures, the month did not start until they could see that small light beam reflected to them. You can work with the New Moon anytime within the first three days—I believe that to be true for all the phases. Feel your way into it.

In my workshops, I say that the New Moon and the Full Moon are the most "magical" times of the cycle. They are like the exclamation points on the end of the sentences that are the Waxing and Waning phases. Any type of positive spell would be optimal at either of these times. Protection spells, road opener spells, magnetizing spells, good luck spells are all fantastic to do at this time. Think: invitation and attraction for the New Moon time. Think: Lodestones, hematite, clear quartz and labradorite. Think: Artemis preparing for the hunt.

This Moon phase is wonderful for setting new intentions, for attracting new people into your life, for beginning new projects, for interviewing for jobs, for invoking more clarity and spirituality in situations in your life, and for simply allowing new opportunities to unfold. It is optimal for prosperity spells, for career advancement intentions, for creative endeavors to formulate, and for love and romance spells. Think of yourself in different ways. Allow versions of yourself to expand in your own mind. Inquire and question. I think of the New Moon time as the Ace cards in the Tarot: seeds waiting to be watered. The Fool and the Star cards come to mind as well.

This time of the month is a great time to reconcile situations from last month, forgive yourself and others, and plant the seeds of hope, faith, and optimism. A good time to ground and think about what you would like to protect. It is optimal to wait for the New Moon to begin projects, as the waxing period of the moon is considered to be favorable for announcing new work. Behind the scenes work, like gathering resources, making meetings, strategizing, and formulating ideas are optimal activities at this time.

If you do nothing else, taking thirty minutes out of your evening to look at the Moon, feel her energy, and write down your deepest desires and intentions during the first three days of the New Moon phase. Put your crystals out on your windowsill or in your backyard to cleanse in the void. When creating a ritual for your New Moon intention, think about what it is that you are ready to get started on or invite into your life. Think about what colors, tastes, sounds, or elemental properties that would look like. Then gather a candle or candles of that color, and set up your altar accordingly with crystals, minerals, photos, and plant life that invokes those desires for you. Maybe your desire invokes fresh tangerines or lemon water. Maybe it summons feelings of lavender and pink rose petals. Or maybe you just cut out a picture of the state you would like. It's your call! Write down your intentions, dreams, or wishes. Then a week later, check in with those during the next phase: Waxing.

First Quarter/Waxing Moon

The First Quarter Moon (often called a "half moon") occurs when the moon is at a 90 degree angle with respect to the earth and sun. We are seeing exactly half of the moon illuminated and half in shadow. I think of the Waxing Moon as a period of time between the New Moon and the Full Moon, but I wouldn't think to do any sort of Waxing Moon spell until at least six days after the New Moon period. The Moon should appear as a Waxing Gibbous. A great time for a Waxing Moon spell would be six to three days before the Full Moon. In fact, during the Waxing Phase I will frequently do three or six days spells, where I repeat the same spell for that time period to build momentum and strength. (You can work a spell for as long as you'd like, I've even known some people who have worked 30 day spells.)

The Waxing Moon aids the accomplishment of any undertakings. If the time during the New Moon was about planting seeds and gestating in hope and optimism, the Waxing period is about putting the pedal to the metal, so to speak, and not only casting spells but acting on it— bringing the work out into the world. Anything that requires hard work, is an undertaking or needs motivation is our focus during this time. This phase gives vitality, courage, and strength. Think of the Magician and Chariot Cards in the Tarot. All the resources are around you. Summon the correct energy and mindset to use them. At this time concern yourself with the external, begin building what you wish to see, hear, and touch around you.

This time period is also good for attraction, amplified success, and fertility. Think of the literal light reflecting across the face of the Moon, growing larger and stronger, gaining momentum on the stage that is outer space. That is the energy that is suggested to embody at this time. Waxing Moon time is also good for flexing your intuition and enhancing your perceptions of the world. Think: form. Think: pushing yourself a bit more than you are used to. Prioritize things that are dear. Build structures, better habits, network, launch your new website or new project during this time. Pyrite, carnelian, tiger eye, are examples of crystals that embody this "get it done" energy.

The Full Moon

At a Full Moon, the Earth, Moon, and Sun are in approximate alignment, just as the New moon, but the Moon is on the opposite side of the earth, so the entire sunlit part of the Moon is facing us. The shadowed portion is entirely hidden from view. The Moon is closest to us, reflecting approximately seven-second-old light from the Sun.

The Full Moon is stuff of legend: humans become werewolves, witches cackle around cauldrons, and people turn into "lunatics". This is the "mother" phase of the maid/mother/crone triple Goddess. Herstorically, this was the time of the month that magic makers would gather as they could see one another and create ritual together under the luminescent spotlight of the Moon. (Remember, this was before electricity—the night was usually very dark.) Herstorically, if you got your period during this time of the month it meant you were a witch. (One theory I read was this was because you could have sex at this time and pregnancy chances were rare.) Your lover could look into your sparkling eyes and adore you, smiling under the reflection of moonlight.

Many intuitives believe this time to be the most potent, the most fortutious time, and the time when our energy and our power are amplified. On that note, absolutely any positive intention setting, manifestation time, or spell setting you choose to do on the Full Moon will be supported. Go big! Dream your heart out! Reach for what you want. Draw down the energy of the Moon and sit with her. This is the time to charge crystals and put rainwater out under the moonlight to use in ritual.

Divination, protection, communication with spirit and other realms are all good aspects to focus on. Downloading information from your guides or ancestors and/or honoring those entities or deities is a good idea under the light of the Full Moon. Channel, journal. Calling in joy, excitement, wisdom, sensuality or other fully fledged components are welcomed. A lovely woman in one of my workshops suggested the idea of gratitude spells. To thank spirit, nature, the universe, your self for all the wonderful things in your life. That idea was so sweet I began incorporating it into my own practice. Appreciation, giving thanks and offerings to your ancestors, guides, and other deities you feel grateful for is a beautiful practice at this time. Things come to a culmination at this time. Pay attention to what is ending or what messages are around you at this time.

During the Full Moon I tend to take time for myself as I tend to get emotionally and energetically overwhelmed. If I do manifestation work it tends to be more grandiose—reaching for outcomes my subconscious mind may not fully believe can be, or things that are very far outside my perceived sphere of influence. I also work long-range manifestations for my life (healthy and happy retirement, etc.) and spell work/intentions for the Earth, the planet, and her health. When creating a ritual for your Full Moon manifestations, think about what would transpire in your life if absolutely nothing could go wrong; if everything you wanted was in front of you, just waiting for you to choose it?

A couple of days ahead of the Full Moon freestyle in a journal or on paper what this entails exactly: what the elemental properties of these things are—happiness, contentment, safety, interest, excitement, health, hope, etc. What are your top goals, how would you feel in your desired state? Now is the time to write your incantation and gather your ingredients. If it is peace you are after, a white candle, quartz crystals, and perhaps lavender and holy basil are some of the elements you wish to be working with. Maybe this ritual would include an Epson salt bath, and working with protective deities to enhance calm and soothing elements.

If it is creative fire and energy, maybe you want red, orange, and yellow candles, sunflowers, red peppers, tumeric and roses to adorn your altar. You could make a crystal grid of carnelian, citrine, and bloodstone. Maybe you want to wear red lipstick, drape yourself in shiny gold garments, and make a glitter drawing of your desire and feeling.

These are just some suggestions. The Full Moon is a great time for drawing in energy, spending time with loved ones, or reconnecting to what it is you want to see happen in your life and embodying how you want to feel.

Last Quarter/The Waning Moon

This is the period when the Moon journeys from Full to New. Casting spells for removing problems, eliminating trouble, neutralizing adversaries and causing harm is most affective when the Moon is on the wane. Protection spells for yourself, your loved ones, home and material possessions are also best cast at this time. It is also a time when our bodies are most susceptible to cleansing, so it is a good time to cleanse yourself through the process of detoxification. Herbal remedies, health issues could be worked on now. This is the time to cut loose toxic relationships, to get rid of old stuff, literally and metaphorically. This is one of my favorite moon phases: one of meditation, recalibration, and letting go. During the Waning Moon phase challenge yourself to get rid of as many physical objects that do not bring you happiness as possible. This phase is about getting things in order that are not in order: paperwork, doctor's appointments, closets. Magick loves a void in order to bring in the new opportunities, thought patterns, and positive people and experiences that will help you. But first you yourself need to get moving and make space for the new! This is the time to do so.

Energetically, you might feel tired. Recognize the importance of quietude. Spend more time resting or sleeping, more time listening.

Banishing and banning energies are useful during this time. It is ok to say goodbye and write that letter you will never send. Forgiving yourself and others, as well as making amends internally are opportune exercises at this time. Rituals could include burning items or pieces of paper, meditating with tourmaline, and asking Kali, Saturn or Hecate for their help. Burying things, and freezing spells work well here.

The Waning Moon also favors forgiveness and release. Going back and examining the past, and blessing mistakes you think you may have made is useful. Thinking about past dreams and desires and reconnecting with any of them would be good during this time. Trance work into the underworld, and examining the subconscious is best to do under the Waning Moon (as well as the Full Moon). This is a also the most optimal time to cut cords and release energetic pulls to other people, places, or past histories. Of course, anytime is a good time to release and close the door on what no longer serves us.

The Dark Moon

This is the period just before the New Moon (about two or three days before leading up to) when any slivers of the Waning Moon are gone. I see the Dark Moon as the Waning Moon most amplified: this is the time for finality. When you know you need to get rid of a pattern, a person, or an unhelpful behavior the energy of the Dark Moon will help you to do so. You may call upon your ancestors or particular deities, crystal or plant energies to help you with this task and to help protect you during this shift.

Calling on the classic crone archetype Hecate, who is the queen of the witches, can really help you with this one. This is the energy of the High Priestess. Picture the 10 of Swords Card. Whatever pattern in your life that needs to end can be finished finally at this time. Brown, white, or black candles can help you with this. Rosemary can aid you as well. Black obsidian can be used for banishing, tourmaline and kyanite for sucking up negative energy and protection, smokey quartz for grounding, and amethyst and rose quartz for gentle love. Crystal grid your room or around the corners of your home for protection.

Write down the negative things you would like help with eliminating from your life. Really commit to working on one or two of these items every day, and ask Spirit to help you with the rest. Know that as you pass your paper through the candle, burning it up, that it will come to pass. You may chant your incantation or poem at this time, and visualize the peace that will be replacing the negative energy in your life at the next full moon. It is also good to program a small crystal or two, to carry with you as a talisman or reminder on what is shifting in your life.

Using an egg with a banishing spell is helpful as well. Break eggs, smash eggs: use them as symbols for things you want out of your life! Go to a crossroads to do this. After you do a banishing spell, always throw out the debris in another trash can—not yours. If you are burying an object or ashes, do so far away from your home, in a place you rarely go to. Put the remnants as far away from you as possible. Salt is a good way to protect yourself during this time. Sprinkling salt around your home and on your door steps will help protect you. Taking lots of salt baths with other herbs like rosemary, mugwort, and lemon balm during the Waning Moon phase can help you release.

Void of Course Moon

When the Moon is said to be "void of course", that refers to a time, lasting anywhere from minutes to a few days, where the Moon is not in any sign. Astrologers (I got my info from *the Mountain Astrologer*) advise to not start anything new at this time, so see this as a sort of resting and hanging out period, as the Moon is not charged in any specific way.

Blue Moon

The original definition is that a Blue Moon is the third Full Moon in an astronomical season with four Full Moons. A normal year has four astronomical seasons with three months and normally three full Moons each. So a "Blue Moon" would be the addition of one.

Recently, this definition has stretched to include a Full Moon that happens twice in one month. This is pretty rare. Usually the months that have two Full Moons are the months with thirtyone days, unsurprisingly.

Super Moons

A super Moon is a Full Moon or a New Moon with the closest approach the Moon makes to the Earth on its elliptical orbit. This makes it appear very large. A Super Full Moon looks about 10% bigger than an average Full Moon. This happens frequently; usually three or four times a year. Tides will be affected, and so might your emotions. Go outside in bathe in her luminescence.

Ways to Work with the Moon

First, get to know her and how you feel during the different phases of her cycle. Go outside every night and look at the Moon. Notice her. Notice how you feel. Talk to her, listen to her. To know what cycle she is in, make your right hand into a semi-circle. If the Moon fits in the crook of your palm, on the right side of your right hand, the Moon is New/Crescent. Do you feel energized and excited when the Moon is Full? Or completely exhausted or wrung out? You can plan any rituals or self-care activities around that. Let your energy tell you whether to take a bath, or cast a group spell then go out partying. If you are someone who gets their period, then your energy might also ebb and flow based upon that. Notice if your period coincides with a particular phase of the Moon. Most people who bleed get their periods around either the New Moon or the Full Moon. Obviously this will effect your energy levels as well.

Look up what phase the Moon was in the day you were born, if you know that info. Does this correspond to how you usually feel during a specific phase? I knew instinctively that I was born during the Waning Moon because I feel so grounded at that time. It felt like home to me. When I looked it up, it was confirmed. Think about your Moon sign. If you don't know it, you'll be able to look it up pretty easily if you know your birth date and time information. Some people I've talked to suggest that your Moon sign could explain where your strengths lie in casting spells.

There are so many different avenues in which to do this work. One way could be simply as a journal, a way to remember what was going on for you each month. Naming and writing are very powerful tools, especially when done by hand. The Moon acts as natural time keeper. As you observe each cycle pass, you can think about where you were at the last one. What were you doing? What was going on? What has changed, and what remains the same?

You can use some of the exercises as prompts for topics to think about in your own life. There are many questions asked between these pages to get you thinking about dreams, goals, ambitions, emotions, intentions, points of view, blocks, fears, etc., in major life realms. Through the year the topics of relationships, self-love and self-esteem, work and career, money and abundance, community, service, and making changes are all addressed and introduced. The idea is that when a little or a lot of reflection and action are taken in each sector then positive change occurs.

It could be a good idea to hone in on your most important desires for each month, season, or even this half year. Pick between one and three main goals and desires, then work a Moon cycle for one of them at a time. You can go back and forth between a couple if one is more practical, and one is more based on internal change.

Looking at the year as a whole expanse is a helpful guide as well. Maybe your ambitions and spell workings start out more long term in January and February. Maybe that begins shifting in March as the ground defrosts and temperatures rise. Or maybe you pick one theme for each Moon cycle and work through that: relationship to self, relationship to others, career/work/worth, family constellations and patterns, creativity, service to community, intuition. Each cycle gives us the opportunity to examine what we want manifested, what external work we have to do in the world, reflections and downloads on greater expansion, and what we must let go of, release, and sacrifice in order to do so. When we address these emotionally, energetically, mentally and physically, true shift will begin to take place. Once done consistently, results will be seen.

Cycles of the Moon, Cycles of life

At a workshop I once gave, I told the participants earlier that day I jotted down a note about utilizing the phases of the Moon. *Cycles of mindless repetition, or spiraling out into freedom?*, I asked myself. We come across the same patterns and themes in our lives many times. They come around and around again. Themes of control, betrayal, ambition, ancestry, thought patterns, reactions, relationships. So easily the mind can be trapped on autopilot. The cycles of Moon remind us that we can process constructively to make positive change and lighten heavy patterns and burdens. Otherwise, we just automatically repeat the same habits, mindsets and perspectives. Then we wonder why our life feels the same. We wonder why we aren't getting results.

Every hardship and challenge can ultimately be received as a gift for us to take our power back and still move forward with love. For us to acknowledge the bullshit, yet not let our core goals and visions get blocked or swayed. For us to remain heartfelt as the machine threatens to break us down. To stay connected to our highest ideals and knowing even as those around us tell us the opposite— this is our evolving journey through this world.

Are you in another repetitive mindless cycle, or are you instigating your spiral into freedom?

Encounters with our inner and outer demons remind us of how far we've come. Bending into our fallibility with kindness and compassion, acknowledging achievements no matter how miniscule. This is what we've got. The march of time is not linear. It isn't a start and finish line to pass through, rushed. It is a spiral. A circle. Touch base with what cycle, what phase you are in. Notice if it syncs up with nature, if your inner is aligned with your outer and what the Moon can tell you each night, as you walk around underneath her.

This is why this work is so potent. If we start our cycle at the Full Moon, we can download, envision, and receive any messages about our life. If we can identify what we want to see happen, during the Waning Moon phase we let go of and release that which is no longer serving us on our mission. During the New Moon, we invite in new ways of thinking and habits, different opportunities to magnetize to us. During the Waxing Moon we dedicate our our energy and take practical steps in service of the goals that our dreams entail. During the Full Moon, we can expand further in our capacity, take stock of where we are, appreciate all that the universe has extended to us and all that we have given ourselves. Try working one cycle in this manner. If you are diligent your world has no choice but to change in some way.

If you are new to magic there are a few suggestions I have for you. The first is to meditate every day. There is no wrong way to meditate. You can meditate for 5 minutes or 15. You can lay down on your couch with crystals in your hands. You can listen to guided meditations, there are hundreds of free recordings on-line. You can do a walking meditation or meditate while walking your pet. Some people I know meditate when they run or stretch. Sometimes I do a flower meditation when I focus on a flower, soak it in, try to memorize it for a set length of time.

The second suggestion is to make an altar. This should be in an easily accessible place for you. A place you can go to every day to meditate, journal, and cast any spells. A place to put any Tarot or oracle cards, pictures, crystals, candles or other magical tools. Some people I know have multiple altars for various things in their home. There is no wrong way to make an altar. You can change out your altar every week, every month, or every Moon cycle. Consistency is key.

The third is to work on loving, respecting, and appreciating yourself. Our level of self-love can at times determine the place in which we are magically operating. Have a check in. Do you think you are a lovable, intelligent, interesting weirdo who deserves every good thing she works for? Or when you sincerely and honestly listen to your core beliefs and feelings about yourself are you a worthless waste of space who is meant to be in the background, only helping others, only meant to have so little? It is totally great and encouraged to wish for material items, external situations when practicing magic. However if it is coming from a fear-based place, if your deep mind believes you can only have so much, then your intentions and magical work will not be very effective or long-lasting. A lot of our core beliefs about ourselves and the world that determine our actions, reactions and behavior were formed when we were very young. It is our responsibility to examine these honestly and acknowledge if they are no longer serving us. It is up to us to take responsibility for changing our core beliefs if they do not serve our highest goals.

The good news is if your self-regard level is not so high, you can work on this. Pay attention to how you speak to yourself. Think about the origins (familial/societal/cultural) of where this criticism or hatred is coming from and question if it is true or not. Choose to be around people who reflect back to you what an incredible person you are. People who are working on themselves, who are caring and thoughtful. For most of us, our thoughts about ourselves can fluctuate between positive and more shadow side. Get to know your shadow self. Listen to her, love them. Think about what the shadow self's needs are. In general, these come from our most basic survival instincts. It comes from wanting to be safe, protected, listened to, loved. For people who have lived through trauma or abuse this can be a huge challenge to unravel. Be kind to yourself as you do the work. Accept and become more aware of all the different parts of your conscious and subconscious; how they motivate your desires, actions and reactions.

The fourth is to take care of your mind, body, and spirit. Get enough rest. Drink enough water. Be conscious of what you are putting into your body. Exercise regularly. Take breaks from work, your phone and computer. Know how you feel best, and attempt to bring that into your life every day. Don't make large decisions when you feel depleted physically. Honor your body and care for it as best as you can. Make this non-negotiable. So many of us do not do this. It isn't easy. Try as much as you can to take care of your physical needs and listen to your body.

Creating and working magical spells are different for everyone. Personally, I enjoy a certain structure that involves preplanning/gathering any supplies and giving myself time, anywhere from one hour to three hours for the actual spell work. This generally includes clearing and setting up my altar, sitting down to write my intentions, writing the actual rhyming spell/poem that feels right. I cast my circle, get in a meditative or trance state, do my visualizations, light my candle, pull any oracle or tarot cards, give any offerings, write anything down, and/or feel an energetic shift. Spellwork is like poetry. Do what feels right to you, what moves your body and spirit.

Choosing when to cast a spell need not be complicated. If you feel like casting a spell, go to it. However, many people feel that spells are more powerful when they are cast during certain Moon phases and Moon signs and as well as during specific days and times of the week. This is because various planetary energies are believed to be more available for use during this time and those energies can add a bit of strength to your own.

A general rule of thumb is to work with the energies of the cycle anywhere for up to three days after the major Moon phase. (This would be the night of the Full Moon up to 2 days after that. Although, I just had a witch in one of my workshops who said she would never dream of casting a Full Moon spell as after, only just a day or two before. Again, spellwork is personal.) There are some practitioners that insist that spells are only effective when they are worked on the exact minute of the exact day of the Moon phase. If that is what you feel like you need to do, then by all means, go ahead. I don't know if I have ever worked a spell precisely down to the minute and my results have been good enough that it has caused me to cast aside my East Coast scepticism and carry on with this type of work unwaveringly.

At the end of the day, this is supposed to be fluid and fun. While working effective magic generally requires a decent dose of discipline as well as every day consistency/repetition, it isn't supposed to feel like something to check off from a to-do list. It is supposed to feel as natural as breathing. Be excited about engaging in ritual and magic. Time at your altar is restorative and grounding. A somewhat effortless collaboration between nature, spirit, and your intentions and energy.

Many of the rituals and spells suggested in this workbook are loose, so as to facilitate taking ownership of your own practice and process. For example, I never include actual rhymes of spells, as I find that words are personal and powerful, and you can create much more meaning out of your own creation. There are suggested affirmations that you may utilize, adjust or practice with.

All of the spells and rituals deal with the season, with the month's themes, with the day, with the suggested astrological archetypes that the particular Moon phase happens to be in. These are researched and gathered for you by myself and my wonderful contributors to offer the optimal suggestions and elements for your own work. The majority of these archetypes and myths that still inform the occult as well as societally are from an ancient time. Many are outdated and archaic. It is on us to create new archetypes, new myths, new stories, to incorporate more complex and complicated truths that reflect our current time. It is our responsibility to question what we read, what we believe, and how we can expand. Cultural appropriation runs rampant in certain spiritual communities. It is up to us to be accountable to ourselves and others to practice our spirituality as ethically and as progressively as we can.

If you find that your own intuition is telling you to do another spell, go for it! Magick, ritual work, and spiritual practice is deeply personal. It is not one-size-fits-all. You do not need spend a lot of money on fancy tools. I've created spells with candles from the dollar store, a pen and paper, and flowers I've picked in my neighborhood. The most important thing with spell casting is your energy, your focus, and your intention. I go into more detail throughout the workbook, with a specific focus on spell-casting in December.

Astrology and the Moon

In Astrology, the moon rules Cancer and the Fourth House, the House of home, and ancestry. The Moon spends roughly 2 1/2 days in each sign. It is feminine energy and it represents our deepest personal needs, our basic habits and reactions, and our unconscious.

What do we feel we need for a sense of security? Look to the Moon in your natal chart for answers. Sometimes the Moon is our shadow side, the hidden parts of our personality; our emotions, the unconscious, our intuition, our spontaneity, and how we make ourselves feel comfortable and safe.

Some astrologers believe it can represent our relationship with our mother or how we mother. Some astrologers believe that when the Moon is in your sign, or falls near your birthday, then it is a "power moon"Likewise, we can use what sign the Moon is to help us with our spell casts and manifestation.

This is just a truncated list to start. There are many books on this topic for you to read!

Moon in Aries: Spells involving power, authority, willpower, self-possession, new starts and renewal.
Moon in Taurus: Spells involving love, sensuality, work, career, investments, physical health, property, and finances.
Moon in Gemini: Spells involving travel, communication, education, networking, new business ventures and connections.
Moon in Cancer: Spells involving home, intuition, spirituality, creativity, emotions, family, and all moon deities.
Moon in Leo: Spells involving authority, strength and courage, joy, fertility, confidence, identity and identity representation.
Moon in Virgo: Spells involving health, craft, education and career.
Moon in Libra: Spells involving legal matters, relationships, harmony, love, beauty, and business partnerships.
Moon in Scorpio: Spells involving psychic development, magic, transformation, sex, death and personal power.
Moon in Sagittarius: Spells involving the written word, integrity, truth, educational matters, motion, and travel.
Moon in Capricorn: Spells involving drive and ambition, politics, structures, career and financial gain.
Moon in Aquarius: Spells involving science, personal choices, leadership, community, the collective.
Moon in Pisces: Spells involving telepathy, clairvoyance, intuition, boundaries, addiction, creativity, past lives.

Each of the 12 signs has their own attributes, colors, energies that we can harness while working spells or manifesting our desires. This is the inherent energy we can call upon which will be revisited later. From a Wiccan standpoint, the Moon as planet symbolizes and rules women, family, magical magnetism and removals, changes, personality, magic, psychic abilities and their enhancement, revealing of secrets, matters of reincarnation, inspiration, intuition, emotional issues, matters of the home, conception, child birth, boats and travel by sea, the force of magical rituals, enlightenment, enlivening of the instinctual feelings of the sub-conscious, renewal of self image, and finding your spiritual purpose.

Moon Colors: Silver; White, blues, blacks, grey

Colors for Candles, Altars, etc.: Silver and white

Crystals: You can use any crystals in spells that correspond to what you are trying to achieve, as well as what you energetically resonate with, but crystals that specifically correlate to the moon are moonstone, clear quartz, bloodstone, flourite, chrysocolla, amethyst, emerald, labradorite, selenite, herkimer diamond.

Days of the Week and Casting Spells

If it were up to most witches, our week would actually start on a Tuesday, then wrap up on Saturday. Sunday would be for fun and adventuring, and Monday would be for more quiet, introspective, home-based activities. If our Tuesdays were our Mondays, I truly believe we would all feel better.

When casting spells, setting intentions, you can tune into the different days of the week and think about what Planetary attributes most make sense for your spell. Perhaps your spell around launching your digital business would be better done on a Wednesday. Again, check in with your intuition, your schedule, and what rings true for you. The seven day week became popular in Mesopotamia then was added to the Roman calendar in AD 321. The planetary correspondences come from around that time as well.

Monday is ruled by the Moon. This day is about the home, dreams, intuition and psychic abilities, the subconscious, family and family constellations, ancestors, secrets, and emotional issues. This day would be best used around water, meditating, writing poetry. The Moon rules Cancer.

Tuesday is ruled by Mars. This day is a good day to work spells on courage, energy, sex, lust, and desire, ambition, victory, overcoming large obstacles, willpower and magnetism. This day would be great to try a new exercise regimen, push harder in a new pursuit, and initiate challenging conversations on. Mars rules Aries.

Wednesday is ruled by the planet Mercury. It rules business (importing/exporting, trade, contracts, networking, communications, the internet), writing and all other forms of communication including public speaking, education and all matters encompassing learning, teaching, skillsets, travel, memory, messages, and intellect. Mercury is a powerful planet as it moves very quickly—lots of spell work can pertain to this planet. Mercury rules Gemini and Virgo.

Thursday is ruled by the gigantic planet Jupiter. This would the day to think of initiating spells on expansiveness, luck, growth, creativity, health, abundance, good relationships, and gain—especially all gain related to wealth, personal identity. Jupiter also rules rewards, honors, accomplishment. This would be a great day to cast spells relating to work opportunities, public perception, and any relationship or business growth. Rethink how much space you take up in your own life and how you might expand even more on this day. Jupiter rules Sagittarius.

Friday is ruled by Venus. This would be an opportune day to cast spells pertaining to love, self-love, unions, beauty, harmony, prosperity, creating beautiful things, growing living things such as plants and communities, divine femme or feminine sensuality and sexuality, and social standing. Venus rules Taurus and Libra.

Saturday is ruled by the ringed planet Saturn. Saturday is a day for working spells and ritual pertaining to karma, karmic lessons, power, control, discipline, ancestral matters, magical power, debts of all kind, wills and other contracts, as well as death and transformation. Saturn rules Capricorn.

Sunday is ruled by the Sun. A wonderful day to cast spells pertaining to self and the world, innocence, recovery, consciousness and truth, deep prosperity, faith, hope and belief, creativity, fame and ego, power, positive will, career, and higher self integration. Sunday rules Leo.

A note on the language in this book: Obviously we know the Moon is not gendered. None of the planets are. Obviously, we know gender is a construct. Obviously, we, as a people want to get beyond binary gender as we know it, beyond stereotyping and bias, into equal reverence for all. Sadly, in 3-D reality we aren't quite there yet. When imagining the Moon, make it feel relevant for you. Your Moon might be Trans. Your Moon might be the Cutest Gay Boy with the Nicest Moustache. Your Moon might be a reflection of your highest self, the one with no gender and every single one of them in one. Your Moon might simply be a cold, dark rock with the amazing abilities to reflect, shapeshift, control the water on our planet. It is up to you!

Much of this project is about recentering and reframing the feminine/femme experience as intregal and central, as it has been ignored, diminished and belittled in our society—an excuse for violence and a way to breed shame. For that reason, I refer to the Moon is "she", "her", etc. Similarly, the word "magic" implies card tricks and slight of hand."Magick" refers to the craft. In this workbook I swap them out freely.

All moon times, moon signs, and moon rise times are Pacific Standard time and are culled from *The American Ephemeris 1950 - 2050* by Neil F. Michelsen & Rique Pottenger, and double-checked on the NASA website. If you do not live in the Pacific Standard Time Zone, this information might be later, earlier, or one day off.

It is suggested that you buy a notebook in conjunction with this book— most likely there is not enough space between these pages for all you may wish to keep track of. Writing by hand is preferred. Writing is a channel of sorts. Writing helps us process. Writing helps us remember.

Here you can jot down some basic wishes you have for the second half of 2017.

Dreams I have for self-love:

Dreams I have for myself and health:

Dreams I have for myself with career:

Dreams I have for myself and community:

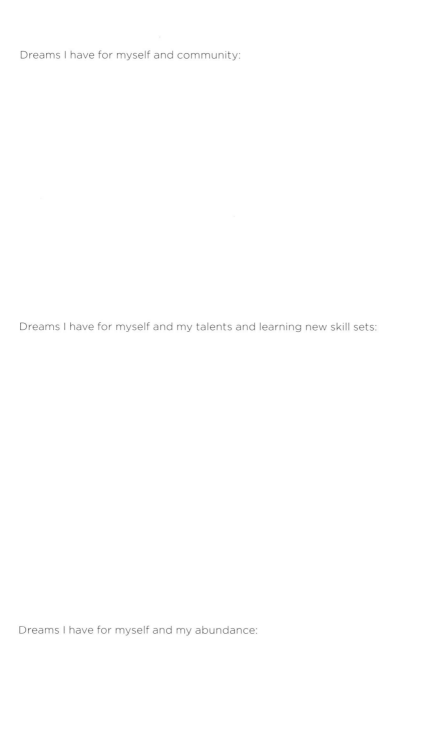

Dreams I have for myself and my talents and learning new skill sets:

Dreams I have for myself and my abundance:

If you have an Oracle or Tarot deck, you might want to take the time to pull cards for each month that this workbook covers.

July:

August:

September:

October:

November:

December:

JULY 2017

JULY 1ST- 7TH WAXING MOON
JULY 8TH FULL MOON
JULY 16TH LAST QUARTER MOON
JULY 23RD NEW MOON
JULY 30TH FIRST QUARTER MOON

In the Northern Hemisphere, July is the month where we allow our gaze to linger longer in the wild. Into waves crashing at the beach, our feet buried deep into hot sand, or on a trail, seeing the sunlight filter though the greens and golds of woodland's walls. When most of us wake up, the Sun is already out, rising just before 6 am. Like the Sun, our Moon rises and sets at a different time every day, rising in the afternoon in the beginning of the month, then rising about 45 minutes later and later each day. See if you can say hello to her in daylight, ask her to give you her messages in the night.

Out in nature, we are more in our bodies, more in the moment. The smells of lilacs and lilies waft through the day into dusk. In the garden, there tomatoes and blackberries waiting to be picked. We dunk in rivers, feeling stones under our feet through the clear, cold water. The sunlight falls upon the water's surface—diamond beams lighting up our pupils. Luckily, there is a slight breeze that rustles through the foliage. All the elements—fire, water, earth, and air—are in easy engagement during these summer months. You may wish to harvest a few treats for your spell crafting in winter. Always ask the plant, branch, or stone. Always leave an offering in exchange, even if it is just a sincere thank you.

Astrologically and elementally, we are transitioning from water to fire; according to tropical astrology the month of July is in the sign of Cancer until July 22nd, the sign of Leo from the 22nd until August 22nd. Water is intuition, emotions, insights, nourishment, spirituality, mysticism, mystery, and flowing creativity. Water is Yin, a cup, a vessel. Water takes on many different forms: ice, rain, clouds, waves, puddles, ponds. A channel that allows raw magic to flow through. A feeling. Fire is passion, energy, inspiration, life force, enthusiasm and excitement. Will and courage. Fire is Yang, a growth, a behavior, an external activation.

The Tarot Card in the Major Arcana that best exemplifies Fire and Water together, for me, is the Chariot. The Thoth deck calls this card "Mars in Cancer". With the red planet of action, passion and ambition in the intuitive and persistent sign of the crab, nothing can stop the Chariot from moving forward into a new paradigm. With the right amount of psychic protection, what could you accomplish?

The origins of the Chariot card come from a more mystical depiction of processions, parades, and other pomp and circumstances that began in ancient times and are still practiced today. Us strange humans still feel the need to revel in public pageantry; while last month was Queer revelry, this month contains those of the political nature. In the United States, we celebrate Independence day. July 4th, 1776 is the day the Declaration of Independence was signed, the day this country ceded from the British Empire to become their own colonialist superpower. Some useful alternative histories of this land are *A People's History of the United States* by Howard Zinn, and *An Indigenous Peoples' History of the United States* By Roxanne Dunbar-Ortiz. In France, Bastille Day is on the 14th, a day that commemorates the storming and dismantling of a prison. Fire water. Illusions of liberty. Consciousness and will.

In Japan, July is also the month when Mount Fuji opens each year to visitors. On July 7th, on the seventh day of the seventh month, one day before this year's Full Moon, some Japanese people celebrate Tanabata, a star festival, celebrating the legend of the union union of two deities in love, Orihime and Hikoboshi. Practitioners hang seven different types wishes from trees, often burned or cast out to sea afterwords. Fire water. Celebrations of love. Wishes and dreams.

This month, we are halfway through the Gregorian calendar. It is one of the hardest years we've witnessed in some time. Our internal circumstances have no choice but to be affected by our current political climate. All of us have had to, and continue to, confront many challenging truths and lessons, individually and as a collective. This month would be an opportune time to revise your intentions, your goals, and ambitions that were made at the start of the year. Recommit to a few that you've put on the back burner to finish the summer and then proceed into autumn, refreshed and recommitted to the whole; and the sum of her parts.

Where is your firewater?

What does it feel like?

How will you use it this month?

Astro Roll Call
By Diego Basdeo

A brief snapshot of the stars for your monthly needs by your one and only lunar dude, Diego Basdeo. For more information on how the planets are working with the Moon go to diegobasdeo.com and check out Lunations, a Moon-focused astrological forecast.

Aries: James Baldwin says we all must respond to our vocation. You must ask yourself not only how do you respond to your vocation but how do you respond to challenges in your work—particularly concerning your reputation and status? The following question you could ask is: how can you creatively influence others and how can you be creatively in service to your community and beyond?

Taurus: If you've been feeling a little selective in the information you choose to take in, consider this: while it is a virtue to be focused, seeing the interconnectedness of things is true wisdom. If you're feeling less than appreciated, it's time to learn new skills around letting people come in and leave your life, however permanent or temporary.

Gemini: Who is putting you in power? Are you a player or a patsy? Take a look at where you may dominate or where you are afraid to use your considerable strengths. There may be some issues around overwhelm and with this month's astrology, it may be time to let something go so something new can come in. As the month builds towards the New Moon, think of new ways to develop your values around self-expression. Be bold. Be receptive.

Cancer: Are you waiting for someone to tell you how amazing you are? How beautiful you are? What incredible work you've accomplished? While validation is so, so important, all shellfish need to come out of their shell sometime and I'm asking you to do it this month. You may just get the praise you so earnestly deserve.

Leo: I see you being able to get a lot done. However, when it comes to HOW it gets done, you might feel surprisingly attached to your methods of work right now. Try to be flexible. Later in the month we see a time to be fully you, uncompromisingly in all of your ways.

Virgo: This is a great time to assess what you're doing with your life and think of how it can bring you joy. Strategize your fun. Later in the month we will look towards levity and light to see how our contribution in the world can or could truly inspire and heal others. This is where real fulfillment lies.

Libra: It is worth it to work on nourishing your family, chosen or otherwise, as a way to nourish yourself emotionally and foster a sense of security through authentic compassion. Ensuring your family does not need for anything creates deep bonds of trust and reciprocity. Careful with projections this month. It is best to be honest with others as well as yourself to establish authentic roles and healthy boundaries.

Scorpio: We need tangible results. Talk to a trusted friend, colleague, or mentor about your work in the month, especially around solidifying plans. Build up your relationships with superiors if you have them, emphasizing mutual aid rather than dominance and submission. Changing the language and the perspective will allow creativity to thrive.

Sagittarius: Folks may be looking to you as a leader these days. It's important to use this time to seek out what you want from the lifestyle you are creating. Broad visioning is wonderful in the beginning but this time is specifically about material security. Counterintuitively, sharing wealth builds wealth. Create channels to let power move throughout your relationships.

Capricorn: Good news! The stars are asking you to relax and retreat. Be with yourself; cave it up. Time to regain a sense of self. Later in the month it could be in your best interest to go back into the public eye, if just to make yourself known as someone who possesses talent, intellect, and resources. Pay attention to the timing of these opportunities, check the circumstances, and make sure the opportunities align with you and those you are working with.

Aquarius: You may be very intuitive and maybe even psychic when it comes to your and others' professional and public goals and ambitions, and your abilities are often your secret tool for gaining extraordinary results. But knowing that in traditional professional circles metaphysics and spirituality are not always welcome, you may hide your intuition or deny them in order to establish and maintain a professional public image.

Pisces: This is a time of organizing your friends. Bring them together for a cause you all believe in. This is a time of incredible power concerning your interpersonal charisma and networking prowess. Identify those around you who can help you in your work. Learn a little about the work that they do and build a bridge. You can surprise yourself with how fun it is to be a community leader when you're doing the work that heals the community.

JULY 1ST-7TH: WAXING MOON

Waxing Moon Magic & Energy Checks

We begin this month's moon phase in Waxing. When the Moon is in her Waxing phase, you may feel more energetic. The light from the Sun on the other side of the Earth covers more and more space on the celestial screen that takes center stage on our night's sky.

Some gardeners use the phases of the Moon to dictate their activities. That is because as Earth's only satellite, the Moon is in a gravitational vortex with the Earth, affecting our tides, and as some people posit, our energetic bodies. (Humans are mostly made up of water.) When the Moon is in its Waxing phase, pruning the garden encourages growth (*The Old Farmer's Almanac 2017*, page 244.) Similarly, according to most witches, it is in the Waxing phase that you want to do spell work around growth and expansion of any kind, including but not limited to: financial gain, prosperity, abundance, community, friends and mentorships, opportunities and luck, love and sex, health, energy and the physical self, the home/immediate surroundings, psychic development and intuition, self-esteem, self-confidence, and new skill sets.

The Waxing period is my favorite time to practice repetitive spells. Spells worked during this time really pack a punch, particularly around form-based manifestation, i.e., objects, dollar amounts, new homes, and other tangible wishes, desires, and wants. High John the Conqueror incense is good for these types of spells, as are orange calcite, honey calcite, pyrite, jaspers, malachite, and the colors gold, yellow, brown, orange, and green.

Repetitive spell work also encourages spiritual growth, awareness, and play. Practicing ritual and spell work—while to be taken incredibly seriously and held in an exalted manner—should also not feel like another chore or something to tick off of a dreaded to-do list. It is encouraged for you, during the Waxing Moon, to sit at your altar for a predetermined period each day. Pray, meditate, cast a spell. Spells should feel like a party for your soul! Repeat the same spell every day, or experiment a bit with the various aspects of each. This might be different from, or in addition to, any morning practices you already have.

Magick and spell working can be viewed as art, and must be practiced and developed—as the magic is in you, and individual talents must be pinpointed and worked with. Maybe creating chants is your major talent, or you feel really confident at making grids and mandalas. Perhaps it is visualization and astral projection you are really stellar at, and you want to work more with grounding techniques or herbs. There is always something new to learn and explore and it is normal to go through different cycles of research, experimentation, and practice.

From a practical standpoint, when we think of the Waxing Moon, we also must think of our physical energy, how that is related to one's emotional body, one's creativity, inspiration, and intention. How well is it protected, where is it flowing, where is it going? This is a wonderful time to take an energy inventory.

Physically, emotionally, mentally, what gives you energy?

What would you like to be doing more of?

What are some ways you can bolster your energy on the daily?

Here are a few ideas around energy to try during this Waxing Moon period.

Do an energy inventory. What sucks your energy? WHO sucks your energy? How can you change this? What is an energy suck or loop that can be broken or stopped? What is an energetic suck or drain that could be outsourced, or dealt with in a quicker, lighter way?

Focus on your energy. In the morning, call your energy back from your dreams, from other realms, from the day before or the week before or the lifetime before. Before you leave your house, put up a protective bubble around you. Carry some kyanite, obsidian, or tourmaline in your pocket.

Set an alarm on your phone for three times a day. When the alarm goes off, do an energy scan. Is energy moving freely around in your body, or is it trapped or stagnant somewhere? Do you need to breathe into your shoulders, knees, or tummy? Do you need to stretch, squat, take a five-minute walk? Is your protective bubble still up? Do you need to call your energy back again?

Take time to take a 10-, 20-, or 30-minute walk around in nature for two to five days in a row. Even if it is just to a street near you with beautiful and interesting trees or foliage. Do you feel particularly drawn to any plants or trees? Do you need to spend more time with this plant? Can you research what it is, what it might mean, see if there is a tincture or a tea that relates to this? Take a moment to find a tree friend and "listen" to the tree. Maybe you want to hug it, place your hand on it, or put your cheek and ear up against its bark. Most trees that are large have been around for much longer than you. Can you feel its energy? Does it have any messages for you?

What I am working on during this time period:

What I need to continue to do:

Solid goals, magickal or practical:

Notes on any spells or activities during this time:

JULY 8th: FULL MOON in CAPRICORN 9:07 PM PST, 7:49 PM PST MOONRISE

Rewarding Forms/Forms' Reward

This Full Moon shimmers out above us on a Saturday, ruled by the planet Saturn. According to *the Old Farmer's Almanac*, the Native American name for the July moon is the Full Buck Moon, or the Thunder Moon. However, in my research I have been unable to locate which Native American people named the July moon this. The Algonquin, who mostly lived/live in southern Quebec and eastern Ontario, call this moon "Squash are ripe." The Cherokee, originally living in what is now called the American Southeast, called this moon "Ripe Corn Moon." There are many, many different names for moons—mostly depending on what was being cultivated in each region, and what was valued agriculturally and seasonally in a region. You can make up your own name for this moon, depending on what you see, feel, hear, wish!

As always, we can work with the cycles of the Moon to suit what we are going through in our present lives. If we are fatigued, we rest. If we are joyful, we must follow our urge to celebrate, clinking glasses filled with ice cubes, fizzy water, and lime, surrounded by the laughter of precious friends. If we are consciously opening up to the dialed-up energy around a Full Moon, downloads might come in, the whispers of ghosts, ancestors, or angels perking up our ears. Messages may come in via billboard, a song lyric on the radio, answering the questions we weren't sure we even had.

If beginning self-work around a new cycle at this time, then this Full Moon might be the time to download and receive messages. Start from a place of acceptance and gratitude, and be honest and clear about what you need. What do you want? What must you sacrifice to obtain your new desires? Treat yourself to a longer shower or bath, and a night of journalling, meditating, brainstorming, and mind-mapping. Reflect on what is true for you now, what chapters need to be closed, what doorknobs are ready to be twisted open. Be clear about asking spirit, the universe, your guides and helpers to come through and offer clear information about your situation that you intend on utilizing in the 3D realm.

From a spell working perspective, this day would be an optimal day for spells around recognition, career, and ambition, including all the dedication and commitment it takes to get one there. Saturn, ruler of this day, traditionally rules structure, karmic debt, financial debt and repayment, fulfillment, discipline, and truth—harsh or liberatory. Anything you feel you are owed—including that which you owe yourself! Remember, you can't attempt to manifest anything that you don't feel that you deserve through and through: from the tips of your toes to the curve of your earlobe. Are you, in some way, giving this to yourself already? If not, it is time to begin.

Yesterday, Friday, was ruled by Venus. If the inclination during this time is to do spell work around beauty, love, home and hearth, or that which you prize or value, prosperity, and relationships (to yourself, and others), then perhaps you do it on this Full Moon eve. Some witches believe that spell work must be done ON the Full Moon, right down to the minute, but this witch is quite a bit looser. I believe it is the quality of belief, will, commitment, and intent that informs the outcome, more than the exact time of a spell. If opening up consciousness, summoning and growing personal power, expanding and growth, or working on improving your health fall into your interests, then you may wish to cast your spell on Sunday, ruled by the Sun.

At this time, pay special attention to whom is paying special attention to you and to what you care about. Who mirrors your heart? Who is showing up for your talents, your self-dedication? Pay them gratitude, in words and actions. Send them love, even if they aren't human.

We can also choose to view this time through the lens of astrological archetypes. When the Moon is Full, the Moon, the Earth, and the Sun are in alignment. The Moon is wholly lit up by the rays of the Sun. Our Sun is in the sign of Cancer, and this Moon is in the sign of Capricorn. (In general astrologically, all Full Moons fall in the opposite sign that the Sun is in.) Our last Full Moon that included the signs of Cancer and Capricorn was six months ago in January. The Moon was in Cancer, the Sun in Capricorn. The prompt and theme in this workbook around that Full Moon was around the theme of self-love. Of devotion to oneself, of unwavering acceptance. You might want to have a heart check-in at this time. In what ways has your self-love deepened? In what ways has it allowed you to feel more free, or continue various commitments? Where might your self-love practice grow more? What are some tangible ways you can give that to yourself?

The constellation of Cancer, the crab, comes from a Greek myth. Hera, Queen of Olympus, sends Karkinos, a giant crab, to hinder Hercules from winning the battle during the penance of carrying out the Twelve Labors. Hercules kills the crab, and a grateful Hera sends it up to the sky. Other ancient renditions of this sign include a scarab (ancient Egypt), a turtle (Babylonia), and a crayfish or lobster (ancient Europe)—mostly creatures with shells who spend their time in water.

For the constellation of Capricorn, "Capricornus" means "goat horn" in Latin. One origin of the myth of this constellation is that of Pricus, the king of the sea goats, immortalized in the sky by Cronus/Kronos (Saturn), the god of time. Another origin is the constellation of Amalthea, a goat that fed the infant Zeus after he was almost devoured by his father, Cronus. Yet another myth I found is the association between this grouping of stars and Pan, the lecherous god of nature, fertility, and the wild. One tale has Pan coming to Zeus's aid in battle defeating the monster Typhon: the goat god dives into a river and the parts of him that are underwater turn into a fish. Zeus immortalizes him in the heavens as Capricorn. Instead of palaces and temples, Pan was mostly worshipped in caves, grottoes, and the woods. As Christianity took over Paganism, anything wild, inherently pertaining to the messy body or weirdly feminine was attempted to be controlled and/or wiped out. (For more history on this, read *Witches, Midwives, and Nurses* by Barbara Ehrenreich and Deirdre English, or *Caliban and the Witch* by Silvia Federici.) According to Rachel Pollack, "the common image of the Devil is simply a mixture of the Greek god Pan and various other competitors of Christ" (*78 Degrees of Wisdom*, pg 111). So is that Devil card in the Tarot really that bad? Or is it an invitation to walk on the wide side? To shed automatic modes of accepting history and our place in it?

The "goat horn" symbol of Capricorn and the "shell/home" metaphor of Cancer ask us to examine and consider what we need to feel at home and protected while scaling greater heights—where we must do the work of diving deeply, so that when our ambition ascends, our subconscious doesn't thwart us and try to drag us down into the muck of self-sabotage.

Intertwining these archetypes is a full examination of the legacy of one's heart and the various forms it can take: untethered by limitations or assumptions, protected by a gentle yet fierce inner knowing, a knowing of the reserves and resources that devotion, commitment, and sacrifice require. At this time, let's take responsibility for our successes as well as our missteps, shall we? Acknowledge what we've run away from, and what the truth of that symbolizes.

What do you care about?

How does this care manifest itself through form?

Where does this care wish to take you, in your career, your life goals, your legacy?

It is time to put down roots. Sink into self-made safety. Gather energy from your networks. Make supporting sustenance your joyful companion: the cawing crow on the wire above your head. Because that is the essence of the base of what you must build if you are to scale great heights. Groundedness, steadiness, and cascades of vibrant heartbeats work as the pavement of dreams.

Get really real with what it is your heart wants at this time. Get really real about the work it may take, shirt sleeves rolled-up style, day after day, to get there. After all, magic is an art form that will not work if you don't. After all, isn't it time to go after what you really, really desire and lay claim to it through dedication and consistent work? After all, if there's anything we've learned so far, it's that there's no time like the present. To recommit, to practice devotion, to write the poem to take out the recycling to call your congressperson and complain to code the website to deliver the vegetables to trim the bangs to paint the protest sign to ask the cute babe out to starting the hard conversation with the housemate to research the course to meditate to call the credit card company to ask for a hug to give yourself a deadline to let yourself commit, really commit, to your own true incredibly precious and imperfect and arduous and heart-stoppingly breathless one and only life?

That is the gift. Commitment and devotion. The follow-through. For the sake of the moment itself only. And in equal measure, to keep going, day after day, tethered to the unfolding and the huge dream in same measure.

Where in your spiritual practice are you devoted?

How I am feeling at this Full Moon:

What I am committed to manifesting at this Full Moon:
How would that feel?

What must I be devoted and committed to in order for my wishes to transpire:

What my higher self knows I must undertake internally around this desire:

What my higher self knows I must undertake externally around this desire: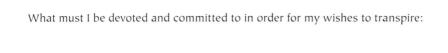

If you do not already have an altar, a place you can go to sit at once or twice a day, please set up a space for yourself to do that. This will act as an anchor. It will make your spell work, rituals, and all intentional time feel safe, secure, and owned wholly by you. For tips on altar-building, you can refer to the introduction of this workbook. If you do have an altar, it is time to switch it out with items that resemble your personal interpretation of this time.

Suggested* Full Moon Spell
Devotion and Commitment: Grounding into Practice

Suggested Affirmation: "My safety is my devotion. My spiritual practice is rooted in care. I ground into my commitment to self, and commitment to spirit."

Suggested candle colors: Green, brown, gold, red
Suggested crystals: Picture jasper, malachite, petrified wood, smoky quartz, jet, onyx, garnet, ruby
Suggested herbs: Nettle, oat straw, High John the Conqueror, roots of any kind you feel drawn to
Incense/anointing Oils: Myrrh, cypress

Other tools: Small shovel, spade, and/or small container, pen and paper, sharp knife or other tool for carving candle

Preparation for this spell: This spell requires you to go into a healing nature space. A back-yard or park will do; it doesn't have to be far away. This does have to be a place that you enjoy visiting, a naturescape you feel intimate with. A familiar place where you feel grounded. On the eve or the day of the Full Moon, take your small container, small shovel, and a journal/notepad and pen and go to the nature spot. Walk around until you reach a place where you feel safe and comfortable. Sit down and connect with the ground. Maybe take your shoes off so your bare feet can feel the Earth beneath you, if that feels more appropriate. Ground, running your energy into the Earth. Cast a circle, a bubble of protection. Call in any ancestors, angels, guides, or animal energy you wish to aid you. Take deep breaths. With your inhale, bring into your feet the supportive, nourishing energy of the Earth. With your exhale, release anything you no longer need into the Earth. Anything that is harming you or causing anxiety, release it into the Earth where it can be composted and used for fresh energy. Take a moment with your breath, with being still. Give yourself time to receive any messages from Earth energy.

Get comfortable and spend time writing about this time, maybe answering the journal prompts.

Now with the supportive Earth energy running through you, write down, in the affirmative and present tense, what you are manifesting at this time. Write it down twice. Fold one of the pieces of paper with your affirmation on it. Dig a small spot in the Earth and bury it. Now ask the Earth if you can take a small bit of dirt from it to take away. Gather a bit of dirt, earth, and/or a plant (always asking permission, never taking too much), and put it in your container to take with you. Thank nature. Thank Earth for supporting your desires and wishes and for giving you support and nourishment as you manifest them. Close your circle.

Go back to your home. You may wish to sprinkle some of the earth, alone or mixed with salt, before your doorstop, or outside at the corners of the land where you live.

Take time to set up your altar according to what you have decided you are committed to manifesting in the next six months, and the next six years. The suggestion here is to set up an altar that feels sturdy and symmetrical, supportive, and balanced. Think about the tools you will need to foster your devotion, and utilize those. In some way that feels appropriate to you, incorporate the earth from your special sacred space in your altar. In some way, use the manifestation you wrote down in the altered state sitting in the fresh air, supported by nature.

*Please note that every suggested spell in this workbook is that: a suggestion. Whether you are a seasoned practitioner, or beginner, the ask of this book is to do what feels right, necessary, and meaningful to you.

Notes on this ritual:

Notes on this time:

Ways you will work on creating safety and space for committment, devotion, and your needs and desires:

Intentions around any release or clearing out during the Waning Moon and Dark Moon time:

Any messages, downloads at this time:

●

JULY 21st-22nd, DARK MOON in CANCER

July Dark Moon: Activating the Portal to the Cosmos of Your Heart

By Adee Roberson

The Dark Moon is a time of healing, renewal and release. In this time we cannot see the Moon in the sky, only the depths of the cosmos that surround. At this time, the Moon is directly between the Earth and the Sun. Here we have the opportunity to gather our thoughts, look within, and heal and process what causes anxiety, anger, and heartache. When we look at ourselves honestly we can truly release what does not serve our spirit. When we release, we make room for what nourishes our hearts.

As an empath and a healer, I have a lot that needs to be released. I am an artist and a massage therapist. I have been doing massage for seven years. When I first began practicing, I saw it as a longterm way to be consistent with my own self-care and healing. My logic is that if I support others in their healing, and they trust me to provide a safe and confidential space, I will be forced to do the same for myself on a regular basis. It has definitely worked and it has been hard work because I support others in releasing grief and trauma. What I have learned from working with hundreds of people over the years is that there is so much that we all have to release, and manifestations of stagnation occur in our bodies all the time.

The main practice that I have around release is through art. Having a self-taught multidisciplinary art practice allows me to channel and transmute grief and negative energy through sound, color, and movement. Spiritual channeling through art is really about being guided by intuition. There is no "wrong" way to create and envision. We live in a society that prioritizes capitalism and institutions that are created to serve and uphold the white supremacist patriarchy. With these systems functioning and in place in most of our lives daily, we can get energetically backed into a corner, and blocked by insecurities, and physical and emotional violence. We have lost touch (or some of us have had our knowledge stolen) with the fact that most pre-colonial cultures used artistic creation as a form of magic, manifestation, and healing. The first piece of art I made under my own vision was a birthday gift for my mother when I was seven years old. I took a wood block I found outside and a found photo of her at the age I was then. I painted the wood green, the same color as her dress in her childhood portrait, and I glued rhinestones all around it. My mom was so happy. When I look back on this work I realize I was connecting threads of my lineage, my ancestors, and healing through this found image and object sculpture. The work was also a conversation about class, because I used what I had to create something priceless and infinite; because it was made with love.

For this Dark Moon I would suggest making a soft altar with clear boundaries, as a way to release and to connect to what nourishes your creative self. If you are a seasoned altar maker then I would go with what your intuition suggests. Think of this altar space as a portal for man-ifestation, meditation, protection, and release. After you create this space, work on a drawing, painting, or writing to place on the altar. You can even a place a photo that resonates with you on it.

To download a mix that was created with this piece and time, go to:
www.adeeroberson.com/dark-moon/

Suggested Affirmation: "I will act on and be guided by the desires of my Highest self."

Suggestions for Dark Moon Altar:

Meditate with the Strength Tarot card.

Place a pink candle on one side of your altar and a black candle on the other side.

Write what you want to let go of on a small piece of paper and place under or beside the black candle. Write what you want to grow and place under or beside the pink candle.

Place pink, purple, and black stones on your altar—like pink tourmaline, rose quartz, rhodochrosite, black tourmaline, obsidian, smokey quartz, or amethyst.

Place one of the Ace Tarot cards on the altar. Ask, "What gift do I want to give myself?"

Notes on Ritual:

Other notes on this time:

Intentions for the New Moon:

new moon
& crescent moon

an invocation
secret magnet mirrors
cheshire cat bright smile flashes across time
a shining black sea with glints of light bouncing off of it
in the rain
Artemis decides to rise again for the hunt
the Fool calls his dog outside for his commencing journey
the first rays of the sunlight filtering through
tree branches in the dawn
the seeds that are planted inside of a happy heart's desire
thunderous hooves like lightning in the distance
the bow pulled back, taut
new muscles, almost defined
the cork pops off of the champagne bottle and
becomes a balloon
moving through the darkness into a deepening of knowing
the whispery voice inside guides you through dark forests, into
a clearing

JULY 23rd: NEW MOON in LEO, 2:46 AM PST, 6:17 AM PST MOONRISE

New Moon, New New

Our only New Moon of July comes to us this Sunday, July 23rd! By now, Summer is in full swing. The heat lays sticky thick on the backs of our thighs. Sunlight soaks into the skin, the blood of berries stains our thumbprints. Nature is bursting around us, flooding our senses. By the water, we lay sunning ourselves like so many lazy lizards, drinking in the heat, letting our gaze soften over the glittering waves sucking in and out over sand. Those of us in the city sweat, hide in the shade, or maybe leave the house more. Bees are buzzing, branches are bending over with fruit: our Sun is putting overtime in by this time in July!

The Full Moon was two weeks ago. What needed to deepen around our commitment to our dreams? We can examine any answers or suggestions that came through for us. Did any answers arise during the Waning Moon time? Any portals activated, any small flashes of wisdom or messages that came your way?

It could be a different way of viewing the situation, rewriting our perceptions—rewriting our expectations! Rewriting, more optimistically, what we know we owe ourselves. Finally. Tenderly. Actively.

At this time, we can think about what we wish to call in that is different. The New Moon is always an opportunity for a fresh start in the dark. It's an ace, a seed dream. Find a bright colored piece of paper on the ground, pick it up. On it are written the words we need to hear in this instant. A whisper of encouragement formulated to land just a touch different. A great big Y-E-S overhead, written in the sky by clouds at the perfect moment.

Time is a spiral. It does not always undulate and shift according to the clock or the calendar, but in weirder, harder-to-pin-down ways. A New Moon meditation takes us into a portal where we meet our future cat who tells us what mountaintop we should leave an offering at, if we choose to close a certain chapter. We run into an old colleague in a random store in an out-of-town place that both of us are just visiting. Time bends as we giggle and recount a silly story—our past connects in an instant to the present. When inspiration strikes, time explodes out. There's the idea, the excitement, the fast-forward movement of a project. Suddenly, in that moment, the next two days are taken over by plans, scribbles, drawings, conjuring. One minute you were driving in traffic, letting your mind wander over the blue noise hum of public radio. The next, a new idea for a novel, an art project, or a simple solution to a lingering problem sharpens quickly into focus.

Time can be bent and manipulated. In spell work, the state of trance takes us into another time zone where there is no time. We are simultaneously in the present, the past, the future, and maybe somewhere else: astral, holographic, our energy zooming through the multiverse.

We also know that time is arbitrary. A touch over six months ago, those of us in the West collectively celebrated the New Year. External events also set stages for fresh starts to unfold. This is why rituals exist: weddings, graduations, baby showers. We are denoting and celebrating large transitions. At this time, I urge you to celebrate a new beginning of sorts. Reflect on what your rituals are around the New Year, a move, or any other major change. Do you go through your cupboard, give away clothes, write an intentions list, call the glowing hearts in your life to tell them you love them? We've lived through two and a half seasons together of this particular year. The Summer Solstice was just over a month ago. Hard to believe, but we are just over halfway done with this bizarre 2017. Is it time for you to spend a portion of today making new intentions, new resolutions? Take an hour or more around this time to check in with your goals you made at the start of the year. Has anything changed? Is it time to make new ones or to rededicate yourself to the originals?

Change starts in small increments. Rituals mark shifts. What tiny or large rituals could you enact at this time to mark a chapter beginning or opening to your subconscious or conscious mind? Get creative—it is New Moon time—we are in the void, the time is now to get different, more creative in your thoughts, actions, movements, words, art. Now is the time for risks, going outside well-trodden comfort zones in both sensitive neuropathways and sidewalks.

How do you set the stage for fresh starts to begin?
How do you prime the pump of the well of personal and private new beginnings?

What can you do that is different at this time? Do you have the bandwidth to seek out a curious activity, like a dance class or haircut—one you've wanted to try for a long time? Do you need to go somewhere you've never been before: a hike, a space, a gallery, or a museum? If casting a spell, can you experiment with a different modality you haven't tried before: a meditation, a breath work sequence, or enticing herb or crystal you've wanted to try out? Try making up a fun fresh chant, reading a new poem, or taking time to sit with, research, and explore a new archetype or philosophy. Sometimes our magical life needs a shake-up as well!

This particular New Moon is in the astrological sign of Leo, the lion. The Sun is in Leo as well (typically, a New Moon is in the same sign that the Sun is in, while the Full Moon is in the opposite—although as stated before, there are exceptions to this). Double fire takes over the skies at this time—annnnnddd it falls on a Sunday, ruled by the Sun! This is an opportune time to harness this incredibly potent fire energy. The element of fire is the element of spirit, of consciousness, will, success, ambition, and drive. It was fire that allowed humans to protect themselves during their evolutionary process: providing humankind with the ability to cook, have light in the dark, and forge metal—turning us into alchemists. Have a bonfire, use sparkler magic or candle magic, burn sage or a piece of paper with your intentions on them. Use sunstone, orange calcite, carnelian. Perhaps pair them with cooling elements as well, to temper the potential explosions. At this time, you might want to do invitational spell work on inviting in growth, attention, attraction, desire, passion, sex, excitement, inspiration, energy, higher consciousness, and good health. Darlings, this is a time to be active. Be active and conscious co-creators with the universe. It's time. You are ready. You've been ready for quite a while, really. Haven't you?

The Tarot card that corresponds with double fire is the Knight of Wands in the traditional Rider-Waite-Colman Smith Deck. This sturdy and daring archetype sits loosely on his rearing horse; he's going places. He's traveling and daring us to travel, too. This card is about confidence, courage, adventure, motion, and movement. This archetype knows "all talk" is boring and quite frankly, is cheap. It is what is *done*, where the body goes—whether by car, bicycle, in wheelchair, or aided by a cane or service creature. We all know by now to trust people not by what they say, but by what they do. Are there places in your life you must move to? Is it time to feel the fear, yet do it anyway? It's time; you are ready. Actually, you don't feel ready, but shhhh. Here's a secret, darling: most people never feel ready. Google it. Look it up. Okay, enough procrastinating. Gather your courage, mount your steed of choice, and do the dang thing if that's what you need to get cracking on at this time!

The Major Arcana card that corresponds to Leo is the Strength card. This is quite a complex card, one we can learn from over and over again. This card speaks on self-growth. It knows our healing is facilitated, in part, by our own unique expression. This card denotes inner and outer strength. It is of the compassionate kind, the kind that knows we sometimes need to step away to get closer. The kind that knows our emotions aren't to be clinched tight and controlled; they are to be patted softly like the cat on the couch next to us. The Strength card imparts that the only way out is through, and if the journey is long, rose-quartz compassion is needed. Let's embrace our fierceness. Let's appreciate our empathy. They are our gifts.

Over the head of the person in the traditional Strength card, there is a lemniscate. A lemniscate looks like an "8" flipped sideways. It signifies flow and containment. We are in the eighth month of this year. The Eightfold Path in Buddhism consists of right conduct, right contemplation, right effort, right faith, right occupation, right resolve, right self-awareness, and right speech. It might be useful to check into all, or some, of those themes.

The last time we saw a lemniscate in the sequence of the Majors was over the head of the Magician, in key number 1, another reminder of our conscious creation and the power of flow. Another reminder that time is a spiral, going around and around, the comet with no end. Another reminder that control isn't really serving us, that all we can really control is our emotions, our consciousness, our responsibility to face our own demons first before we can move on to the collective's. An aspect of the Strength card I like to point out to clients is about the choice we have in constructively working with our fears and to what lengths we need to follow them. We have a choice to drop the story. It isn't easy, but sometimes that's the most correct answer. Sometimes we have to move through our pain and our suffering deeply to alchemize it into helpful lessons, to make the howls subside to sniffles. Other times, we can act like our spirals are a dog trying to eat our socks: no good will come of it. We can tell our mind to "drop it!" as we would a pet doing something naughty. If you've been trying to shift a bad habit or inner pattern, gaze at the Strength card and ask your inner voice to tell you what it needs. Does it need to go deep, therapy style, or does it need to dance it out? Do you need hypnotism or breath work, or is it a case of dropping narratives, and replacing those with something else tied to the physicality?

The last Tarot card that corresponds to this New Moon is The Sun. Leo is ruled by the Sun: the heart of our solar system, just 92 million miles away from us. The giver of life to all forms on Earth, it is the main sequence star, just over 100 times larger than our planet. The connection between the Sun and the Earth drives the seasons, ocean currents, weather, climate, and more. The Sun summons the explosion of consciousness and a shed skin. It is the third card away from the end of the Major Arcana. Old paradigms have faded; our consciousness has broken through towards freedom, adventure, and the true joy that exists so purely when we are seen honestly.

At this time, you may wish to meditate with any of the above-mentioned cards. What resonates, symbolically or vibrationally about any of these in particular?

Where in your life do you need to shine brighter?

Where do you need new energy or adventure?

What projects need nourishment, focus? What internal fires need fanning?

This is the first of two New Moons in a row in lovely Leo! This might be the opportunity to hit the acceleration on matters of energy, passion, inspiration, courage, and heart-centered matters. Be careful to pace your energy and be careful to check your ego during this time; too much fire leads to burnout and depletion. Likewise, be mindful of others' flare-ups for the next month: August is likely to be a hot month, not just weather-wise, but in our interpersonal connections.

What I am ready to attract, call in, step into:

What new themes are coming up for me at this time:

How I will enact those in my daily life, language, relationships:

July New Moon Tarot Card Spread Ritual:
Welcoming the New New

Suggested Affirmation: "I act on my own affirmation. The universe supports my conscious creation."

*If you are doing this ritual as part of your spell, simply fold it in after you've done your main spell work (trance state, visualization), and before you've closed your circle.

If you are doing this ritual by itself, take time first to arrange your altar with items that symbolize what you are calling in at this time. Light candles, stare at the flame, breathe, and get comfortable before pulling cards.

You may wish to pull out the cards that correspond with this New Moon time—The Sun, the Strength card, and the Knight of Wands card—and arrange them in front of you however you like. You may also wish to pull out a card that symbolizes what it is you are ready to call into your life at this time.

Shuffle your cards, focusing on your breath and what you are ready to call into your life at this time. When you are ready, pull your cards and arrange them in front of you.

Card 1: What in my life is ready to be manifested during this cycle?

Card 2: How can I call this in effectively?

Card 3: How will this be expressed in a way I can see?

Card 4: How will this be expressed in a way I can feel?

Card 5: Where must I focus my energy?

Card 6: What activities do I need to focus on more, and what must I do differently?

Card 7: What must I let go of, in order to move forward more quickly?

Card 8: What will a possible outcome be if I take these conscious steps?

Keep the cards up on your altar for at least one day. You may wish to keep them up longer, visiting and visualizing with them for a week or more. Happy New Moon!

What my intentions are at this time:

What my spell work entailed:

How I will move forward on this, mind, body, soul:

Transforming Energy, Composting Energy

"Nothing is absolute. Everything changes, everything moves, everything revolves, everything flies and goes away." —Frida Kahlo

The First Quarter Moon comes to us on a Sunday, two days before the month of August begins. (This year, most of the months begin with a Waxing Moon.)

A question that sometimes arises when I give workshops on Moonbeaming is what if the suggested/traditional energy of the Moon cycle does not align with where your body, mind, or spiritual self is? During this Waxing Moon—while the energy is ripe for growing, working later hours, networking, going outside your comfort zone in relation to your New Moon intentions—what if you feel like garbage? What if a case of the slippery sads slithers around your soul?

Well then, my gentle reader, this would be an optimal time to think about composting—your energy, your thoughts, the pains, and obsessions that rattle inside your bones and zip around your sensitive neuropathways.

In the words of everyone's favorite German Jewish theoretical physicist Albert Einstein: "Energy cannot be created or destroyed; it can only be changed from one form to another." All natural energy has the potential to be transformed into something different. Think of the seed becoming the cherry tree becoming a flower becoming a cherry getting eaten by the bluejay who poops out the seed which lands in another State that becomes another tree eventually. Or the decaying body of a dead deer, eaten by vultures and wolves, who use it as energy for their days, then the calcium turning to nitrogen and dissipating slowly into the loamy soil, feeding the worms and the bacteria, and giving way to a fertile canvas ripe for burdock, dandelion, lichen, and endless green to grow on.

There are many different ways for us humans to transform the different forms of energy in our own lives—through art forms, physical movement—to compost energy. The metaphor of the Phoenix rising from the ashes here is pertinent. The phoenix is a mythical creature, living for hundreds of years at a time. The bird would build its own pyre, set itself on fire, and a new bird would rise from the ashes. Ancient Egyptians correlated their god Phoenix with sacred royalty, reborn anew into a soul flight.

During this Waxing Moon time that begins in the sign of Scorpio, we can practice composting our energy. Sensitive people, if caught off-guard and ungrounded, sometimes perceive energetic and verbal communication physically. A rude comment goes into our body and roils around. A lack of response can feel like a burning hole eating up space in our heart. We can transform and transmute this energy. If someone is cruel, we can turn around and utilize that energy into positive, kind communication to someone else. If someone says something hateful or insensitive to us, we can take the extra time and energy to be slower and gentler with ourselves and others. If during this time you find yourself affected by the negative words or actions of others, think about neutralizing or transforming the energy that's embroiling you. Turning rage into a new song, flipping perceived or received callousness into the most meticulous collage.

It might also be useful at this time to revisit some narratives about yourself, or shameful stories about past identities that are holding you back, trapped in a time period you are no longer physically in. Take those dusty skeletons out of the closet, maybe figure out what they were symbolizing, to burn them down and see what bursts out of the ashes. Maybe dress them up with a jaunty hat and a string of pearls. Can you retell old stories, seeing what you've learned, how they've changed you for the better? Can you transform tales of pain into love letters of redemption and knowledge?

Time and time again in this cycle—in the spiral that is the circle of the Moon, the ebb and flow of the tide, the changing of the seasons—the ask is not to just see the "good" things as "good," or the "bad" things as "bad." Or the ending, or the answer, or a reward. Why? Because this can trip us up into if/then thinking. This can tip our focus solely on the external.

During this First Quarter Moon that begins in the sign of Scorpio—that sign of the scorpion, the eagle, and yes, the phoenix—face the fire and rise again.

What is my go-to response when negative energy comes my way?

How can I improve on this?

How will I work on transmuting different forms of energy in my life?

What are some old, unhelpful narratives about my identity that I can transform?

What are my goals for this week:

How I will achieve these?

Neutralizing "Bless It" Meditation

This can be done seated or laying down, as long as you are in a comfortable position. Sometimes you might want to do this while walking or standing. Whatever works for you!

Take a few measured breaths in and out. Slow your breath and balance your breath so that your inhale takes as much time as your exhale. When you inhale, as much as possible fill up your lungs with air, pushing your belly out. When you exhale, exhale all the way down to the bottom of your breath.

Now, imagine your exhale expelling unwanted energy down into the Earth, releasing it so that it goes down into the layers of the Earth— deep into the center's molten core— becoming composted into a different, more helpful form. Perhaps this energy is in the form of a color. Perhaps this energy can be described, has a tangibility, tarriness, or stickiness. Perhaps you have to consciously detach from this energy to let it go. After a few rounds of release, do an energy check-in. Do you feel lighter? Does more need to be released?

On your inhale, imagine the life-giving, resourceful energy of the Earth coming up and rejuvenating you through the soles of your feet, grounding and supporting you, giving your cells sustenance. Maybe this energy is in the form of a color. Perhaps it can be tangibly described. Let this energy go all the way up into your body, your lungs, into the crown of your head. The energy cascades through your arms and hands.

Now, with your inhale, bless a helpful situation. "Bless this apartment," "Bless my body," "Bless this breath," etc.

With your exhale, bless a stressor. "Bless this bill," "Bless this layoff," "Bless this fear," etc.

Do this for as long as it takes for you to get out all the blessings on your current situation. Take a few more breaths. Maybe you want to make a few loud sighs, shake your body out, or release in another way to close the exercise.

Notes on this month:

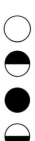

Intentions on the next:

AUGUST 2017
AUGUST 7th: FULL MOON LUNAR ECLIPSE
AUGUST 14th: LAST QUARTER
AUGUST 21st: NEW MOON SOLAR ECLIPSE
AUGUST 29th: FIRST QUARTER

August is heat and sweat. Humid air rustling grass. August is slow days, sticky backs of knees. August is Leo and Virgo: Fire and Earth! Bonfires on the beach and digging fingernails into dirt. Sunflowers, salvia, and dahlias! This month, during Pacific Standard time, the moon rises in the afternoon, starting around 3 o'clock, and cycles further and further, rising later and later during the day. The New Moon appropriately rises at 6:00 am in the morning! This August is an Eclipse month and Mercury is in retrograde for part of it.

The month starts out with the Pagan holiday Lammas on August 1st. Also called Lughnasadh, for the Celtic God Lugh. He was the god of skill and correlated with fire, as he was raised by a smith. Symbols of this holiday are grain, corn, and bread. We can think of honoring Ceres, goddess of agriculture, fertility, and harvest, at this time.

What in your life is ready to be harvested?

What is ready to burst forth, to come through?

From a lunar perspective, this is a big month as both our New and Full Moons are eclipses. Increasingly, a very large amount is written about eclipses, mostly from an astrological perspective. (I've written about them extensively in the previous workbooks, you can always refer back to those.) Astrological events are never to induce fear or panic—this only exists in our minds. These reactions take away our autonomy, our control. Metaphysical pursuits are never to be twisted into another ruler in our lives. We can use insights as more tool-kits and resources for our self-development. Letting anything control you takes away your empowerment and alignment.

Act after pause and inquiry. Pay attention to your cycles as the Moon cycles through the sky, showing us whatever it is we wish to see— whatever we our relying on, the reflections shine us back into ourselves. There might be the impetus to go within, to finish out old projects and follow through with some ideas you've had earlier in the year. Now would be a great time to do so.

The Full Moon Eclipse suggested ritual is one of connecting to our spiritual guides. The New Moon eclipse ritual is one of finding light in the dark. The Waning and Waxing suggested prompts are for shedding, and for affixing spiritual practices to the everyday.

In this world we can have it all: just not at the same time. This month might be a time to think about sacrifices. What parts of your identity, certain goals or cycles must you must close the chapter on? What do the pages of the next chapter look like?

If it is time for you to forgive, turn the page.
If it is time for you to say goodbye, say farewell and turn the corner.

Begin by taking stock. Open up to your interior insights. The ones that resonate and ring true just for who you are now, and who you are blossoming into.

If it is time for you to set the stage for welcoming the new—the magnificent—begin by clearing out the shed. Dust off the light fixtures, and make space for another beginning cycle. Decay and bloom sit next to one another on the shelf. In-between each are our conscious coffins. Any new cycle begins with tenderly laying to rest the previous.

This isn't the month for teeth gnashing control. This month, try not to hang on too tightly. Loosen your grip on the wheel. Remember we are all in process, all in change, at all times. Meditate on the Strength card, and what soft power and head-to-toe empowerment means to you personally. Pay attention to messages, patterns, and themes in the air and how this shows up for you. If it is time to work through any of those, this month would be an opportune time for doing so.

Try to go easy on yourself and others. Your love can be firm and resolute. Your love does not have to look sticky sweet and nicey nice. Sometimes this looks like goodbye. Sometimes it looks like letting go or letting others go. Love circles back, we must be patient with ourselves and others. As the August-born visionary James Baldwin wrote: "Love does not begin and end the way we seem to think it does. Love is a battle, love is a war; love is a growing up." This month, lead with love.

Astro Roll Call
By Diego Basdeo

A brief snapshot of the stars for your monthly needs by your one and only lunar dude, Diego Basdeo. For more information on how the planets are working with the Moon go to diegobasdeo.com and check out Lunations, a Moon-focused astrological forecast.

Aries: How can you make what you do significant in service to others? What risks can you take, politically, intellectually, or metaphysically to get in touch with a larger purpose? There is a call out for you, Aries. If you're having trouble hearing it, spend some time with children or performers.

Taurus: To act on the material plane, you have to act with authority. Authority can be associated with being in the spotlight but because privacy and emotional security are also important this month, there are other ways you can be just as effective. Spend some time helping others connect with the resources you possess. This will encourage them to seek you out and give you a reputation of being knowledgeable and helpful. The goal here is ultimately peace of mind.

Gemini: No time to be locked in now, Gemini, nor is it a time to lock anyone else down. You could prioritize getting some intellectual fresh air this month. It's a good month to immerse yourself in something strange and unfamiliar for the sake of scholarship and reason. Keep doubt at the door and experience the strange.

Cancer: This month you walk the line between material and emotional security. It's a good time to ask yourself what security means to you. When everything is stripped away, what security do you find within yourself? How can your material possessions enhance that? Who can help contribute to your material security, interdependently?

Leo: Find a partner in crime and charity, in spotlight and set design, in comedy and tragedy. Most of all, find a partner who is into you no matter what season, health, or mood you're in. Be mindful and invest in those who are with you when the lights go down. Your generosity is a precious thing and there is only so much one person can give, so choose carefully who receives it from you.

Virgo: Health and service. When erratic hours, needs for material security, and a service-oriented heart come together, this can lead to hardcore burnout. If the mundane things fall behind, it's okay, but be sure to keep an eye on how much you're working so you can be in it for the long haul.

Libra: Host a dinner party. Seriously. Actually, throw two dinner parties. Or at least attend them. It is important for you to remember that it is fully expressing your individual self that gives you your role within a social circle; your uniqueness is what makes you belong. Don't forget that you are a necessary piece in the big picture of humanity.

Scorpio: Your security and confidence with your close friends will come up as a much-needed strength to bring that confidence out to the world. Note the energy your closest people bring to the room and carry it with you. You may end up channeling your own uniqueness and gain a new perspective on what you contribute to projects and social scenes.

Sagittarius: Start with talking. Take in new information without judgment. This will naturally develop your understanding of your own creative percolation and from that, a higher truth can emerge. End with writing, archiving, and researching.

Capricorn: Power, money, sex. There's no shame in the game; these are a part of our daily lives whether we like it or not. Keep in mind, these things work in cycles. Feast and famine. The oldest laws in the book. People rise and fall every day. Keep these in mind in your exchanges this month.

Aquarius: This month is a strong month for developing unique relationships that enhance your personal creative and intellectual perspective. Start out the month social and constructive and develop your relationships through the ways your unique identity can enhance theirs.

Pisces: You may be very sensitive to group dynamics right now. Be mindful of your empathic nature right now. You may process others' emotions without knowing it or lose a sense of who you are in a collective. Misunderstandings can be easy to come by. Choose actions, avoid reactions. If you can't, make art.

AUGUST 7th: FULL MOON in AQUARIUS 11:11AM PST, LUNAR ECLIPSE in AQUARIUS, 11:22AM PST, 7:55 PM PST MOONRISE

Happy Moonday and welcome to the Full Moon of August!

It is a Full Moon, on a Monday, ruled by La La La Lovely Luna herself. It is full on 11:11 in the morning; make a wish! Make three! Then a partial lunar eclipse starts ten minutes later. Be still. Take 11 deep breaths, all the way up from your toes to the top of your head.

The Moon brings up so much. Actuals and metaphors, the perceptions of a perception of a perception. She is everything and nothing, all at once—she can be a cipher, a channel, or a container. She's the mirror that reflects everything in the world and a subversive alchemist: showing us the rays of the Sun channeled through space and time. She's a catalyst, a potent prompt, or an extra in the background. She makes me consider how we are talking about the concepts, granular and abstract, of time and interiors and emotions and gravity and energy and water, and the Earth and the elements and worshipping them and working with them. She shows how we, too, can be everything and nothing all at once.

She makes me think about darkness and light. And everything in between.

With an eclipse, we can't not talk about light and darkness, about the obscuring of both, across the universe's vast stage. Lunar eclipses occur between one and four times a year, when our Earth's shadow blocks the Sun's light, which otherwise reflects off of the Moon. There are three different kinds. This will be a partial eclipse, visible in Europe, Africa, Asia, and Australia. Think of this as us (Earth) and our shadow, falling across the Sun (the self, life), as shown on the surface on the Moon, the mirror to us all.

During this Full Moon, we can't not think about the collective, for one of the archetypes of Aquarius, the water bearer, is one that serves the collective. The Sun is in the sign of Leo, which is ruled by the Sun, the sign of the self. Here we are, trying to rise up into our best selves that can weave the most dangerously compassionate, enduring, uniquely creative webs into the world.

The Tarot card that is associated with the sign of Aquarius is The Star: one of the most beautiful, comforting cards to receive in a reading. The Star reminds us that to heal ourselves is to heal others. When one truly decides to live out the larger project of one's life authentically, this ripples out in service of the collective. What gifts are you giving? What life projects are you ready to begin at this time?

It's a sparkling summer moon, when we are more apt to be outside, our bright eyes opened later and later by the heat and sharp stars, glittering pinpoints in the sky. The *Old Farmer's Almanac* calls it the Sturgeon Moon, but this Full Moon is also called the Corn Moon, or the Grain Moon. We've just begun August, a month about harvesting, honoring the Earth, nature, fire, and communing with sunlight. Some Pagans call this Moon the Barley Moon: this was the traditional time when grain was harvested. What is ready to be harvested in your life now?

The most trusted Witch teachers I know do not advise working spells around eclipses. Why? The energy can be volatile, too much unknown hurtling down the slide at the playground, too many messages ping-ponging around the ether. Now might be the time to rest, relax, and receive messages. To recognize, honor, and give thanks and gratitude for all that you have, and all that is coming to you. You might want to spend a few hours writing down and speaking out loud all that you are grateful for in your life. You could light a candle, slip into a bath, and thank yourself for all you have accomplished this year. You could spend time writing beloveds thank you postcards, telling them exactly how wonderful you think they are and why, or sending encouraging letters to anti-fascist politicians or progressive organizations you admire.

The daring amongst us might want to use this eclipse energy to throw ourselves, slingshot-like, into unknown arenas, to take a giant energetic leap. By all means, if it is time for you to do spell work, go for it. Only you know yourself.

The suggested activity in this workbook for this lunar eclipse is to spend time with your guides—our internal messengers. Spirit guides, that is.

Lots of times, when I try to explain spirit guides to people it gets a bit difficult. My lovely grand-father, a quite open human, asked me, "So you are referring to your higher power?" Well…yes…sure…sort of…

Everyone has spirit, spirit guides, helpers, fairies, ancestors, animal guides, nature spirits, angels, and yes, your higher power, helping them. At the end of the day, it does not matter what you call them, as their aim is the same. These messengers are literally just here to help, asking nothing in return, except for you to live out your most authentic life, fulfilling the specific destinies you came here to experience and work though.

My spirit guides most certainly help me and are most definitely operating in the realm of my higher power, which is to say they vibrate at a higher frequency than myself in my body, which is to say that sometimes their messages are not as much concerned with the how, with the details, with the mundane. Spirit guides can be very big-picture—at times too large for my brain to wrap around—and quite frankly are not always interested in explaining the minutiae of detail. Maybe they've not been bothered with the task of having to be in a human body for quite some time. Being able to have access to, listening to, and enjoying life with my guides has given me joy and contentment that is nothing short of priceless.

Angels and guides come in all different forms. Some come in dreams. Others in meditative visions. Some show up as voices that you can hear inside your body, but are not you. Some show up as sensations; the hair on your neck stands up, certain parts of your body are energized and tingle as if by an outside force. Sometimes the temperature changes; you might get colder, or hotter, depending. Some people I know interact with spirit as physical objects, or animals: a feather in their path, a lizard on a branch, the line from the song on the radio that rings out clear as day, that person you needed to run into just in the nick of time, right before you needed that job or that roommate lead or that solid affirmation. Maybe Spirit comes through to you in animal communication, through the Earth, while meditating with crystals, listening to music, playing music, painting, running, swimming or submerged in water, taking a shower, or hugging trees. There is no cookie cutter way to receive messages from your guides, but there are no limits to how to access them. Other realms are around us at all times.

A friend accesses Spirit by scribing: she writes down the words her guide needs her to know as an intuitive. Some find messages in tea leaves, pendulums, scrying in crystal balls or pools of ink, through Tarot cards, Ouija boards, candles, chanting. Sometimes people have to close their eyes or only be alone to receive messages. Personally, my guide comes in a number of ways—as voices, as a sensation (always in similar areas of my body). Messages may be very, very specific, or a bit more abstract. The trick is to listen and to be aware of messages coming through. It might sound like you. It might BE you! Your inner voice, your inner spirit. You from a different time, you from the future. The point is to act on these messages.

The majority of the very first edition of this book was channelled. Looking back, I cannot remember consciously the great bulk of the information that came out. Spirit very clearly told me I was to write this book in workbook form, and I was to do this for three years. Honestly, gentle reader, I didn't want to do it. I know this might be hard to believe, but growing up as a child my dream was not to be a Moon workbook self-help writer. By now, I've had enough experience listening to Spirit and my guides to know to trust them. So, because it felt clear, and because it felt right, without asking the how/the what/the why, I listened and I acted.

Are there any recurring messages coming through to you that you must act on?

What are some messages that have been coming through to you— for weeks, months, or *years*, that it is time, post-eclipse, to act on?

We can also call our guides our muse, or inspiration. Artists sure do. Real artists also know they never run out of original, personal ideas, because they are close to Source. They curl up their ears to Source, promising to listen, and Source promises that if they use the ideas Source gives them, they will never run out. These artists don't repurpose other images on the internet, plagiarize others' words, or trace other artists' work. Why would they? Spirit has their back, and Spirit always comes through. They make their own. They create their own. The universe has assured them, much like the overflowing rivulets of healing water in the Ace of Cups, that the more they give of their true self, the more they will receive. The water bearer in the Star Key pours out her water, her inspiration, her offerings, knowing that is a part of her healing process and her magical power.

Is it time to get out those images, ideas, sentences have been knocking about in your brain, your journals, underneath your eyelids? Time for the world to see?

Channeling certainly comes in different forms. An entity may overtake one's body, changing the vocal patterns and physicality of the reader (think Whoopi in the movie *Ghost*). Frequently, when I channel, I do not remember exactly what is being said during a reading. I'm there, but the messages coming through are just that: coming through my body/voice/communication. While I mentioned the first time I wrote the book as coming through very quickly and easily, last time the experience was quite different. I knew intuitively I had everything I had to say, but it felt a lot more like work. Sometimes cultivating inspiration takes work. (Think: 8 of Pentacles card.)

Where have you slacked on cultivating your inspiration? Do you keep a journal or folder on your computer desktop where you write all your ideas down? Is it time to revisit this, to force on yourself time and space where spirit/inspiration can come through?

Part of cultivating messages and Spirit is working with them. Messages come through to everyone as a gift, and part of the gift to the greater consciousness is sharing them. Because, gentle reader, the purpose of Allah, or Diana, or Kali, or Jesus, or Buddha, or Ishtar, or Hecate, or Archangel Michael or your late great Aunt Rose or other guides that come through with no names, the purpose is to help the collective. To use your energy, your body, your unique gifts, talents, and charisma as a conduit to serve the greater good. The human collective is more vast than you could ever know. More invisibly intertwined than you could ever see with your naked eyes. The grid of light, hardship, love, and loss that weaves us all together. The domino effect of inspiration and wordless collaboration that is endlessly more important than the money in your bank account, the amount of "likes" that have been counted on the internet, or how many pages of unpaid labor your artist CV goes on for. It is real and it is vital and some people call it "soul" or "authentic" and that's the point, really.

Your guides are here to help with all this.

Hands down, across the board, one must be relaxed to access Spirit. Breath work and meditation help with this. In *Power of the Witch*, Laurie Cabot introduces the reader to the alpha state. In *Opening to Channel*, Sanaya Roman also gives many step-by-step instructions in how to access messages.

If bolstering connection to Spirit is something of no interest to you, then at this time, reflect on you + we. I + us. Pinpoint what you need to cultivate to get your voice out there stronger, to touch more people with your love. Reach out to a group or non-profit you've wanted to help out, do research on ways that your talents can help others. Connect with people you haven't seen in a while. Maybe, together, you can do a tangible activity that will create positivity for the whole.

How are my unique gifts of service to the collective?

How am I of service, daily, weekly, in an ongoing manner?

Does my community need to take up more or less time, space, and energy in my life?

What is my unique gift to the future of the planet?

Is this connected in any way to my own healing?

Where must I begin acting around those gifts?

What other messages am I receiving at this time?

What doors do I feel are ready to opened, and which chapters are ready to be over?

What must I facilitate, in terms of mind, body, spirit, to do so?

How can Spirit, my guides, nature, or my community help me?

Where can I reach out for help or support?

Accessing Spirit/Spending Time with Your Intuition

Tonight, the night of the Full Moon, or perhaps the night before or the night after, the invitation is to open to Spirit, to channeling, in whatever way resonates. Maybe you are well acquainted with your guides, maybe you've never explored this.

Suggested Tools: Paper, pencil, candle or candles of your choosing, oracle cards or Tarot cards, pendulum, other preferred tools
Herbs to Facilitate Opening: Mugwort, blue vervain, holy basil, angelica, lavender
Suggested Crystals: Apophyllite, moonstone, Herkimer diamond, labradorite, quartz crystal, ametrine, celestite, azurite, chrysocolla, kyanite

Make sure you are alone and turn your phone off. If you have pets, you might want to put them in another room. You may wish to put on soothing music and have a pencil and pen nearby. If anything pops into your head as you begin your meditation, you can jot it down. This also helps to further clear your mind. You may have a pot of tea, and anoint your temples, wrists, or throat with your favorite tincture.
Find yourself in a comfortable sitting or lying down position.
Close your eyes.
Focus on your breath, lengthening it and slowing it down.

Feel any stress melt out of your body on the exhale.
Focus on bringing in clear, higher energy on your inhale.

Visualize bringing in red colored breath and moving it around your 1st energy center.
This is the area around your sacrum, the root of your spine.
This energy lights you, and anything there that needs to be released leaves with your exhale.

Visualize bringing in orange colored breath and moving it around your 2nd energy center.
This is your sexual organ area, right under your belly button.
This energy lights you, and anything there that needs to be released leaves with your exhale.

Visualize bringing in yellow colored breath and moving it around your 3rd energy center.
This is your gut and solar plexus/core area.
This energy lights you, and anything there that needs to be released leaves with your exhale.

Visualize bringing in green colored breath and moving it around your 4th energy center.
This is your heart and lung area.
This energy lights you, and anything there that needs to be released leaves with your exhale.

Visualize bringing in blue colored breath and moving it around your 5th energy center.
This is your throat and neck area.
This energy lights you, and anything there that needs to be released leaves with your exhale.

Visualize bringing in indigo colored breath and moving it around your 6th energy center.
This is your third eye area.
This energy lights you, and anything there that needs to be released leaves with your exhale.

Visualize bringing in violet colored breath and moving it around your 7th energy center.
This is the area right above the crown of your head.
This energy lights you, and anything there that needs to be released leaves with your exhale.

While still breathing deeply, call in any helpful guides you wish to speak to. Welcome them in in any form. Notice if anything changes, if any symbols, words, sensations, sounds, temperatures, or colors come in for you.
You may ask them any questions you would like, or ask them to show you anything they would like.

Again, notice if any words or sentences pop up for you.

Spend as much time here as you would like.
If you want, you might want to write down anything that came in while you were meditating.
You may ask Spirit to help you with pulling a card or two around a question you have at this time.
Meditate and spend time with this altered energy, with your journal, pendulum, and your other magickal tools, including yourself.

Remember to thank the helpful energies that came in, and affirm that you are listening and are ready for more messages as the time comes.

Notes on Ritual:

Notes on intentions, manifestions at this time:

AUGUST 14th: LAST QUARTER MOON in TAURUS 6:15 PM PST, 12:18 AM PST MOONRISE

"If one changes internally, one should not continue to live with the same objects." —Anaïs Nin

Sacrifices and Surrender

Welcome to the August Last Quarter Moon! This Monday, we are seven days to the next New Moon, a solar eclipse: the bracket to the set of eclipses that started way way back in February. Seems like years ago, doesn't it? For some of you, it might feel like yesterday. Sometimes, this Last Quarter Moon can act as a time of integration, rededication, and recalibration. One can refine and act upon any messages or information downloaded around the Full Moon time. For those of you who follow retrogrades, Mercury went into retrograde yesterday. In these work-books, we've spoken at length at how much or how little this might affect you. At the very least, give yourself more time and mindfulness around technology, travel, and communication. Practice patience with yourself and those around you.

Last Quarter Moons are most visible during the late night and early morning; setting around noon. Looking up tonight on your nocturnal walk, connect with the Moon. Is the light coming from the top or the bottom? Can you stare in silence at her, marking various shadows on her surface for your memory? Does anything come through to you, maybe through the cricket's high serenade, the nighttime warbles of nightingales?

Sometimes I like to compare this time of the moonth, this balsamic time, with getting your affairs in order before you go away for a long weekend, or even a longer vacation. What is it about knowing we are about to go on a journey that propels forward the urge to wrap up many things in our lives? Think about the cosmic journey you are wanting to be on right now. Knowing, with certainty, that you will not fail in following through with your goals and lofty ambitions, what needs to go? What needs to get taken care of, put to rest? Where can you close that chapter, put that book back on the shelf? Take stock. *Take stock, then act accordingly.*

This Last Quarter Moon falls in the astrological sign of Taurus. Taurus is associated with the body, with physical sensuality, with earthly delights of all sorts. This archetype asks us to think about how we embody what we value, as well as what we assign value to. Massages, perfume, false eyelashes, labradorite crystal balls, poetry books, relationships, a fridge full of food, electric cars, feelings of freedom, works of art, vintage T-shirts, art supplies, random thrift store finds, ceramic pots for our seedlings, the space to explore our needs. What is in your life for you to enjoy and what could be cleared out, reconfigured? This sign is also commonly associated with work and working. What are we working towards, what are the hours in our day doing for us long-term, for those around us, for the greater collective, and for the planet?

This archetype's shadow side asks us about examining our own stubbornness, or particular forms of black-and-white thinking. What are we being stubborn about letting go of, and why? Is it simply habit? Or is there something deeper as to why you can't let go of certain relationships, ways you speak of yourself, behavioral patterns, addictions?

Manifestation does not work without sacrifice. We must accept, resolutely, that the old ways, old things, old sayings, old actions, will not march with us triumphantly into the future. They will not create a different future, the one we've been aching for. "The Master's Tools Will Never Dismantle the Master's House," Audre Lorde reminds us (*Sister Outsider: Essays and Speeches*, 1984).

What are you prepared to give up, to clear the way for something different?

Consider the King and Queen of Pentacles. The King of Pentacles is fixed Earth. Yes, he is the master manifester to be sure. Look at all he owns in his card! Is he ruling all his objects, or are they ruling him? This card can sometimes be about control and a deep need for security as evidenced by having more than enough on the Earthly plane. At this time, you might want to revisit what trappings of the material world are just that: trappings. Too much desire, too much greed serves no one, least of all yourself. We've seen, more and more, how damaging and far-ranging and devastating greed truly is.

Compare this archetype to the Queen of Pentacles. She's water and Earth. The Queen asks us to think about our relationship to abundance, what feeds us on a nourishing level. What is it that sustains us? She needs fewer things and more time. Less stress and more space, joy, and nature. The King of Pentacles derives his pleasure from what he owns and has, and the Queen derives her power from knowing that all she owns and has is inside of her already. When the Queen of Pentacles pops up in a reading, I think about what is luxurious to me. How do we define freedom and being truly fed? Most of the time, it is the things that money can't buy that are priceless and beyond capitalism: time, emotional and personal connections and experiences, joy and play, connecting with nature, and the energy of our own creation. (I'll write more about scarcity and abundance, things, money, and magic, later on in this workbook.)

Unless you've either won the lottery or are blessed to come from a trust fund, you need to consider both the King and Queen of Pentacles as forces in your life. Are these archetypes in balance in your life currently? Is it time to spend more time in one realm for a while?

I want to briefly touch upon sacrifice in magical workings. In some spells, we give up objects as a marker, as a testament to the seriousness of our sacrifice. We burn physical pieces of paper that are stand-ins for what we are ready to let go of. Certain practitioners work with their blood or their hair—literally parts of themselves. Starhawk suggests using the idea of "eco-spellcasting," that is, using materials in your spells that can only decompose, i.e., only natural materials and herbs. I do believe that when working spells around releasing and letting go, that it is helpful to declutter the various physical objects in one's life, as many of us are very visual and physical creatures.

During this week, this pre-New Moon week, prepare. Clean. Clean out. Clear. Clear out. Get rid of objects that are no longer serving you, that do not fit with new visions, different goals. Your workspace, your desk, the files on your desktop. Rearrange the shelves, the medicine cabinet. Mend what needs to be mended. Repair what needs to be repaired.

What have you been putting off dealing with?

Where can certain stubbornness slide into something more flexible?

Where is there stress, and can it be abated in an easy way, in an unstressful way? (Sometimes the solution is treating the issue in a different mindset and energy with which it was originally created.)

Think about a snow globe, shaken: the snow globe of your life. So many different items, so much stuff. Can you make all the snowflakes feel more intentional? Do you need to rearrange some items in your snow globe? Are there different ways to feel less disruption or distraction?

What is getting in the way?
Is it stuff?
Obligations?
Certain relationships?
Your own blocks and procrastination?

What I am working on at this time:

What I am wishing for during the New Moon:

What needs to be dealt with, or given away, gotten rid of, so that this can be invited in?

Any notes on ritual, spell work:

Notes and intentions for Waning Moon times:

Full Solar Eclipse
29*Leo
Dearly beloved:
We are gathered here today to get through this thing called life

by Jessica Lanyadoo

A full solar eclipse is when the Moon fully occults the Sun. Historically, this was seen as a bad omen as the Sun's light was totally overshadowed by the Moon. It's terrifying to have reality, as you expect to see it, change up on you. During a solar eclipse, darkness blocks out the light; this is a time when the needs of the heart can overshadow one's sense of self.

This makes it a prime moment for transformation and heartfelt openings and a bad time for hiding from your demons. Solar eclipses are like New Moons on crack, and their energies are felt and integrated over a period of approximately six months. We are being called to work with what we're feeling as deeply as we can. It can be tempting to focus on the surface of events, but there's a bigger meaning underneath the surface that the eclipse is trying to call our attention to.

This eclipse is a part of a big astrological doomsday prediction that I won't detail here. This is the first full solar eclipse to be visible across the USA for almost a century, and astrologers have been writing about it for a while. The whole US will share in this transition, which has profound implications in these intense times. The eclipse will be exact at 29 degrees of Leo, which is the last degree. When planets hit this degree their energies are especially potent. The issues that get triggered now can easily feel like crises, so it's good to set up a support system if possible. The eclipse hits the astrological chart of the good ol' USA right where it hurts: in the heart. The future is up to us, so we must get activated, get involved, and be loyal to the causes that matter most to us. Leo is all about the power of participation, and when emotions are repressed and unfelt, and power drives are submerged and not pursued, there can be an emo flood when the damn breaks. Leo is also the sign that governs royalty, so we may see a collapse or rise in power within our political system. Whatever happens on this date, its reverberations will be long felt in this country and in our personal lives.

Sabian Symbol Exploration

Astrology gives us so many insights and ways to geek out on healing self-analysis. Sabian Symbols are visual representations for each degree of each sign of the zodiac. A clairvoyant woman named Elsie Wheeler originally channeled them in 1925, but the astrologer Dane Rudhyar popularized them with his 1936 book *The Astrology Of Personality*. These symbols are meant to signify the spiritual embodiment of each degree of each sign, and can be used as a powerful catalyst for transformation. The full solar eclipse is at 29*Leo and the Sabian Symbol for this, according to Wheeler, is:

"A Mermaid Emerges from the Ocean Waves Ready for Rebirth in Human Form"

Rudhyar wrote:

"Mermaid awaits Prince who will make her immortal"

With their ability to live deep in the water (the realm of emotion) and to transform shape, mermaids have long been symbols of feminine energy. The mermaid is also a meaningful symbol for many trans females. This symbol is that of femme power and its ability to transition from land to water and back again. It's the power of femininity beyond genitals, and it's power without brute force.

Rudhyar was a visionary and so I choose to believe that when he referred to Mermaid awaiting Prince he meant Prince: the high-heeled, gender-bending, artist-formerly-known-as, and not some BS dude on a horse. Prince was a rule-breaking, sexy MF who fought for his rights and the rights of others. He was the embodiment of an introverted extrovert, who had a dynamic public life but also a private life of activism and charity that he sought no accolades for. In fact, Prince had the 29th degree prominently placed in his birth chart.

This is an opportunity to meditate on the creative force of divine feminine energy in one's life, or in the world at large. This energy is not delicate; it's fierce. It's not responsive; rather, it's the very force of creation. This Sabian symbol calls for revolution in the name of love, art, and transformation. To be in the ocean is to be with the depths of our emotion—both the conscious and the repressed. To emerge from it, as the mermaid does in this symbol, is to take that emotional self-knowledge from the depths and integrate it into the mundane life.

The energy that flows from the heart *is* immortal. It is light and sound and vibration. We must birth the selves we wish to be and the world in which we wish it to live. This planet does not belong to us, but we are meant to be its stewards.

Stars & Stones Ritual: Securing Safety In The Dark

This ritual is intended for honoring those who are lost, whether they are trapped in material situations or mind-frames that limit or harm them. Use it for lighting the way for stealth, and securing safe passage for those who need it.

You'll need:

-*A bowl (anything except plastic will do)*
-*Water*
-*A pinch of Epsom salt*
-*A small candle in white, yellow, or orange*
-*A pen that doesn't work or a nail*
-*Prince music (optional)*

▲ Get a large bowl with a small amount of water and go into a private room for this ritual. Before you begin, take time to meditate or connect with your Guidance. This is a time to share your light with others caught up in dark places, and if you are to illuminate them, first you must be lit up, yourself.

Visualization

▲ Find the light that resonates with you. I recommend that you connect to the minerals and gemstones deep in the Earth, or if you prefer, you can connect to the stars above. Resonate with their limitless light and channel it throughout your energy body. Fill yourself up, breathing calmly and deeply. Listen to any messages you receive and honor the gift of your interconnectedness by passing this energy along.

Ritual

▲ Charge the water with both hands by running light and love energy from the center of the palm of your paws into the water.

▲ Now put a pinch of Epsom salt in the bowl. This will help to ground your intention.

▲ Get your candle and inkless pen or nail for the candle. Carve your intention into the wick in multiples of three. Write as much as you like—the purpose here is to engrave your intentions into the wax. It doesn't need to be legible, and messiness is encouraged.

▲ Place the candle into the bowl.

▲ Sit. Be calm and still. Reconnect with the light of the stars and stones and feel the light bright within you as you light the candle.

▲ Say a prayer for the safety and happiness of those you intend to reach.

Leo loves to party like it's 1999! Listen to your favorite Prince music if that lifts you up. This ritual is not for fame or glory; the service offered is from a place of abundance and the bright light of love. Do not take pictures of, or live-stream this ritual. It is meant to be beautiful and fierce but also private. Act from that place when you light the candle.

When channeled with intention, joy and play are as powerful as solemnity. Once your ritual is done, dance with only the light of your candle if you feel called to it.

Eclipse Affirmations through the Signs

Aries
My power to adapt allows me to grow at my own pace.
Taurus
There is enough room for everyone's success.
Gemini
My voice is a powerful tool, and I can use it to heal.
Cancer
Dance and movement help me channel my connection to the Divine.
Leo
I am a creator; I determine what I am willing to experience.
Virgo
I honor my future with a willingness to change; I release the things that are no longer serving me.
Libra
I am open to the flow of my life; I can learn from any life experience.
Scorpio
Collaboration helps me to build my dreams without my ego getting in the way.
Sagittarius
I give to others from a place of abundance within myself and am fed by the act of giving.

Capricorn
"A ship is safe in harbor, but that's not what ships are for." -W.G.T Shedd
Aquarius
I am willing to carry the responsibility of my wisdom and privilege.
Pisces
I am willing to see the truth of the dark and the light.

Notes on ritual:

What my intentions were:

Other notes, dreams, messages:

Where the Practical Meets the Spiritual: Small Spells for Higher Vision

"Once you accept time and space as real, you will consider yourself minute and short-lived. But are they real? Do they depend on you, or you on them?...Behave as if you are pure aware-ness, bodiless and mindless, spaceless and timeless, beyond 'where' and 'when' and 'how'..."
— Sri Nisargadatta Maharaj (*I Am That*, pages 241 – 244)

Happy First Quarter Moon! We are officially about eight days away from our next Full Moon. The energy now might be described as zingy, ramped-up, slightly wired, optimistic, and carnelian courage called in. The fire theme continues on in this month, as the Moon today is in Sagittarius, and Tuesday is ruled by Mars, the red planet of action, desire and lust, forward movement, and aggression. If you've been tracking your daily energy levels/moods in the back of this book, you may have been noticed some patterns. If this Waxing Moon phase is one of ramped up activity and stamina for you, take a moment to write down a list taking this into account. Is it time to spend an extra three hours at work a few nights this week redoing your website or reaching out to like-minded people to show your work to? Maybe it is time to implement a new physical activity regimen or incorporate more psychic hygiene, like meditating in the morning or at night. This might be the moment to begin some changes to guide you through the rest of the year.

At this time, think seriously about bigger pictures, bigger visions for yourself, as the light from the Sun begins to fall over the surface of the Moon—taking up more and more space over this symbolic subconscious mirror. This surface of basaltic plains—called oceans and bays and marshes and lakes—are really topographic features. The ones that named them were men, hundreds and hundreds of years ago, and they named them breathtakingly dramatic titles such as the Lake of Luxury, the Marsh of Decay, the Seething Bay, the Sea of Clouds, the Sea of the Edge, the Serpent Sea. These differences in the Moon's surface are easy for us to see, due to the craters made by meteors landing and crashing into our little Moon, which has no atmosphere to protect it from the hazards of space. Only twelve humans (all men) have ever been lucky enough to plant their feet on the Moon's surface.

At this time you may wish to examine some ways to bring higher focus and vision into everyday life. You can see the surface of the Moon from your car window, so why not bring your own further-ranging plans front and center into the dashboard of your life?

It is all a dream, this cosmic joke or sacred arena called life, so focus on higher thoughts. We are what we think, we are what we do, we are how we handle. One very easy way to fold magic and spell work gracefully into your daily life is by attaching it to activities and small rituals we already do every day. That way, the far-out visions are reigned in closer, more tangible, tethered to our habits and activities. Small spells, when worked consistently, can be very effective.

If you take a shower every day that would be an optimal place to do a variety of small spell work. Visualize the water coming down from the shower as a rainbow, cleansing your physical and energetic body. Imagine all the mucky grime, the unwanted energy, going down into the drain, down into the Earth, to be recycled anew. Rub a salt scrub over your skin and imagine new thought forms and energy coming into your reborn surface. While brushing your teeth, name what you are grateful for, including things that haven't happened yet, but you are sure are coming.

In the morning, before you sit at your altar, cleanse the room with sage, Palo Santo, or other burning herbs. Be mindful that you are clearing out any stuck or stagnant energy, and that you are calling back your own energy.

Before you leave your house, check in with your auric bubble. Does your aura need to be zipped up a little tighter, a little closer to your body? As you cross the threshold of your home to go out into the world, bless the day. Carry a piece of jet or tourmaline in your pocket or purse. Bless all the information you will receive from the outside world, bless all the lessons that are waiting to be learned, and look forward to receiving information and guidance from spirit. Tell the elements you are grateful to them, that you will pay extra attention to how they show up for you.

Before you sit down to work, visualize yourself working smoothly, tension-free, easily with little distractions. Imagine what certain priorities you have in your day-to-day work that most encapsulate where you would like to be in a month or a year, and commit to finishing those before the work day or week is up—see yourself in the spiral of time, embarking on a few activities this week that will get you closer to your core career goals. Before you go to bed at night, ask for any stress and strain or tension to be removed from your body. If you have a problem you are struggling with, ask for answers to come to you in your dreams, or to be waiting for you in the morning as you sit at your altar. In these ways, you can bring spirituality into your own routines. Magic begins weaving itself into your life, little by little.

Research a few herbs, perhaps ones that are special to your family background, or ancestors' history. Research their nutritional and metaphysical properties. Bless them, work with them various times during the day, invoking their power. Work one or two of them into your cooking intentionally. Put one or two of them on your altar, in your wallet, or in your pocket. Drink a tea made of Holy Basil and meditate, focusing on your breathing and heart. Spearmint is great for clarity of thought, abundance, and luck. Mugwort, the herb that is the most associated with the Moon, the witches' best friend, is traditionally used for clairvoyance and invoking psychic trance or astral projection.

Rosemary is another very accessible plant helper for witches. She helps with protection (during the Middle Ages, people hung rosemary around their necks to shield them from the plague), loyalty, for cleansing and purification (put her in salt, add to your non-toxic cleaner with lemon to clean surfaces and floors in your house), for protection from nightmares (you can put a sprig of rosemary under your pillow, or by your bedside table), and to keep moths away (by putting a sprig in dresser drawers and closet).

Some witches believe rosemary is good for making one more memorable to others, and studies have shown that rosemary stimulates the memory center of the brain. You can use rosemary oil to increase circulation by massage. Some witches associate rosemary with the Moon and Aphrodite (the herb's Latin name, Rosmarinus, means "dew of the sea"). For more information on practical and magical uses of different herbs, some places to start are *Healing Wise* by Susun Weed, *The Master Book of Herbalism* and *A Compendium of Herbal Magic* by Paul Beyerl, *The Gift of Healing Herbs* by Robin Rose Bennett, and *Herbal Healing for Women* by Rosemary Gladstar.

Many times I've spoken about repetitive spell work during the Waxing Moon. Manifestation around ramping up, expansion, growth, health, and abundance flows perfectly with the Waxing Moon. This is an incredibly opportune time to do spells that last for three, five, or even six to nine days. Doing this repeatedly also trains the brain that this is what is happening: if a weak spot for you in your magic is doubt or disbelief, you might want to focus on repetitive spells. (This is also why I chant my spells over and over again, so it becomes an accepted and graceful loop in my brain.) Generally, the first day and the last day are the days in which the spell work is longer. The days in between are the days I continue implementing the spell with chants, lighting candles, and visualization.

Remember: a lot of this is a strange dream, our mind processing and making sense of past, present, and future. So much of what we negotiate, navigate, and perceive are illusions created by past hurts and experiences. By now, we all can be certain that it is the time to stay high-minded with our thoughts, deeds, words, and actions. Practicing small spells throughout our day can keep our perspective on what vibration we intend to enact. That, in turn, reminds us that the universe is working in tandem with our considered actions.

Let's point our best selves forward, as high as a flying arrow catapulting into the clouds, moving to different terrain, propelled by our awareness of the past, and not accepting less for our best vision of ourselves and greater humanity.

A few ways I can weave magic into my life this week:

How I will do this:

What I am working on manifesting during this Waxing Moon:

What thoughts and affirmations, actions and deeds will aid me with that:

Any other notes on spell work, energetic work, herbal or crystal magic I am experimenting with:

Notes on this month:

Intentions for the next:

SEPTEMBER 2017

SEPTEMBER 6th: FULL MOON
SEPTEMBER 12th: LAST QUARTER
SEPTEMBER 19th: NEW MOON
SEPTEMBER 27th: FIRST QUARTER

September is a month of preparation and progress. Sunlight is still abundant, autumn's promise begins taking hold little by little. Between the first major harvests of the summer and the last of October, the fruit is still on the vine. In the beginning of the month (around September 7-9) are the Feast days of Oshun and Yemaya. Oshun, also spelled Ochun, is the Orisha of rivers, sensuality, and love. Yemaya, also known as Yemanya, Yemoja, and other various spellings, is the Orisha of all creation, the great mother. She gave birth to the moon, stars, and the oceans. Think of creation, think of switches turning on this month.

This month, traditionally, has been the month of beginnings. Most schools in the United States start by September. The Jewish New Year is this month; the same date as our new Moon. The Islamic New Year, Al-Hijra, is on the 20th. This makes sense, as both religions are lunar-based. The Autumnal Equinox is just a few days later: summer is officially over. Then, just after the Equinox, some Witches observe Mabon; the feast of the harvest, a celebration of all that we have, in spite of the dark, or, perhaps because of it.

The suggested exercises for this month cover transformation and vibration (making sun-and moon-infused flower essences around the Full Moon), thinking about what parts of yourself you need to shed, and invoking acceptance and gratitude for your health and body (a ritual for the New Moon). During the Waxing moon there is the encouragement to go forward, to move ahead.

Get really clear about what it is you want, moving forward, and then do the darn things. In the words of bell hooks, who was born this month on September 25th, and whom everyone should be reading, listening to, and invoking: "What we do is more important than what we say or what we say we believe."

What have you been saying you are going to do for ages? Is it time to suspend any paralysis and just do?

Where is your talk just talk? Where are you walking towards, and why?
This month can be a month of decision making and change making, after we've gotten clear from the reverberations of last month's eclipses. Moving into this month, think to yourself, "September will be the month I _____ . "

The Moon keeps spinning, counterclockwise around the earth, no matter what. The orbit of the moon is almost exactly the same distance as its' orbit around Earth, so we see the same side of her. Day after day, eon after eon, she spins, she gleams, she glows as if she is light herself, with no one she can hear cheering her on, helping her out, telling her what to do or how to do it. She still shows up, on her elliptical path all the same. As if by magic, controlling the tides, so much transformed light reflecting right back down to us.

This month, be the Moon.

Astro Roll Call
By Diego Basdeo

A brief snapshot of the stars for your monthly needs by your one and only lunar dude, Diego Basdeo. For more information on how the planets are working with the Moon go to diegobasdeo.com and check out Lunations, a Moon-focused astrological forecast.

Aries: I'm not sure the word surrender is in your vocabulary, but this is what I'm asking you to do. This is so counterintuitive to you but necessary for deep change. "As above, so below." Getting in tune with a higher power also puts you in tune with your inner world of material and physical health.

Taurus: It is a social month for you, dear Taurus. Attract the people you actually want in your life. People will be watching you and will learn how to treat you by how you treat yourself. Please be kind to yourself. This might get a little under your skin when it comes to inviting people into the playful hobbies you usually like to do alone. Remember the childhood rule: if you can't say anything nice, tell them to get the fuck out your house.

Gemini: How are you being called to contribute to society? I want to tell you that through your work you will confront a few sticky spots from your childhood. The idea of contributing to a whole might bring up your role in your family of origin. This is a chance for you to have a say in how that all plays out.

Cancer: Broaden your scope; experience the unknown as possibility instead of fear. Take up all the space and encourage others to do so as well. There is room for all of us. Take rigorous notes of all of these possibilities and study them like bright stars over an ocean to new lands. The more you understand them, the safer your voyage, but you cannot begin to understand what you don't know until you venture outside of what you already know.

Leo: You need to trust your intuition. Transforming yourself may require some big sacrifices, but where those are only you can know. No one else. Whatever it is, make sure you have the basic needs you require locked in.

Virgo: Transformational relationships through radical cooperation. Explore imaginative and selfless parts of your relationships right now. Take into consideration all others and identify yourself in the milieu of your most compassionate contemporaries.

Libra: Work may get a little "far out" this week. You may be pushed to be more generous with your time and energy this month. While you do have a lot to give, remember your personal mantra of balance. Give AND take. And not necessarily in that order.

Scorpio: It's time to have a little fun in the stratosphere, babe. Get silly with your serious ass. What nourishes the sore spots of everyday harshness we experience? Late into the month you may recline back into your shadows. Think of this month as gathering information somatically to put to use intellectually. Fun can be just as serious and deep as pain. Pain can be fun, too.

Sagittarius: Phone home. Pick up the phone when the call is to come home—even if they call collect. Especially when they call collect. You don't have to "go" but at least give it a listen. Your rep may get a little jostle and it will help to be well rooted in knowledge of where you come from.

Capricorn: Talk the walk and walk a lot. Open up that broody brain. Sharpen your wit on the stone of philosophy. Discourse is the word, and it ain't a bad verb for your month. Take a little trip to a strange place, metaphorically or otherwise. It may bring you some much-needed insight.

Aquarius: Money is a means to an end and for you it means that there may be a reality check about how important those means are to you. This is a learning opportunity to explore and undo mythologies about how you keep your house and your future in order. Material wealth has a tax, but so do the means in which we get this wealth. Think about what secrets you may be keeping versus what privacy you may want around material possession. Make sure that when you receive cash or valuables you are clear on the strings attached.

Pisces: While you are no stranger to people taking advantage of your generosity, your desire to give and the recognition of how much you give and take may be out of whack. I suggest reeling back the care smorgasbord and saving a little for yourself. Allow thankfulness from yourself and others.

SEPTEMBER 6th: FULL MOON in PISCES 12:03 AM PST, 7:45 PM MOONRISE PST

Welcome to the only Full Moon of September, 2017. This Full Moon takes place on a Wednesday. Mercury has just come out of retrograde—for those of you who make note of such events. With this moon smack dab in the middle of the first proper week of the month, we have the perfect opportunity to reflect, assess, emote, feel gratitude, charge our crystals, write down massive manifestation dream lists, enjoy time with loved ones, take a salt bath, go out dancing, have awesome sex alone or with someone else, light some candles, and snuggle up with what we wish to accomplish this month.

We have four months left of the year, including this one. The year has a quarter left in it. We are two weeks and two days until the Autumnal Equinox— that divide that connotes the cascade into proper fall weather, even if by now we can start to feel it, a chilly premonition. This moon is sometimes called the Harvest Moon—when the Moon, closer to the Equinox, stimulates the harvest, staying brighter to help finish all harvesting chores that sometimes have to continue on into the night. This year, the Full Moon in October lies closest to the Equinox, so it is technically not the Harvest Moon. This September Full Moon is also called the Corn Moon and the Wine Moon, describing that time of the second harvest, after August's. What is ready to be harvested in your life, brought up and left out for you to enjoy?

When the Moon is full it is reflecting the maximum amount of the Sun's light. Something within us is stirred. For some, this glare from our subconscious is too strong—we shirk, spiral into shame, are overcome by emotion. Our energy sapped by disillusionment, a bottle set adrift in the ocean with no message for the finder.

For others who know what they want, who are clear about their purpose and core, this time is excellent for further illumination. Now can be the time to come back inside, away from the noise and distractions. Any messages or inspired illuminations spark the fodder for later external manifestation. Write down, dance out, paint any and all inspirations that come through around this time.

In terms of spell work, we know the Full Moon is the most potent time for casting spells for anything one feels drawn to: manifestation, guidance, protection, energy raising, abundance, creativity, fertility, psychic messages and awareness, closure, peace, harmony, support, and alchemy are all supported at this time. The Moon itself is alchemy and fertility; she transforms reflected light into illusion. Her surface beams out the light of the Sun to become a lighthouse in the dark.

If there is something you would like to see manifested before or during winter, now would be a wonderful time to do so. This Moon is in the astrological sign of Pisces: the cosmic fish, the last sign of the Zodiac. Spell work that is especially favored now is for creativity or creative projects, potions and elixirs, fostering intuition or psychic ability, mental health, humanitarianism and collective efforts, faith, vulnerability, facing and healing psychic wounds and fears, facing the past and moving on, and accessing other planes—developmentally, emotionally, spiritually, and psychically.

Pisces, a mutable sign, represents the last sign of the three water signs—that time period when we are preparing for a change in the seasons. Think back to the last time we had a major moon phase in Pisces: that was our New Moon eclipse at the end of February, just over six months ago. Looking back, were any cycles initiated for you? What has transpired and manifested in your life since then? Remember, naming all that you have accomplished and cultivated, no matter the scope, is a way to keep manifestation going. Remember: naming all that you are in the process of accomplishing is a way to keep your goals in perspective, even if they haven't become tangible form yet! These are simple ways to touch base and communicate with your intuition, and the universe, that the wheel is still turning.

Greek, Persian, and Sanskrit names for the constellation of Pisces all translate to "fish." Fish, coming from the life-giving element water, were traditionally sacred to the Moon-goddess. The glyph of Pisces also resembles a crescent and waning moon. (Barbara G. Walker, *The Woman's Dictionary of Symbols and Sacred Objects*.) In the traditional Rider-Waite-Colman-Smith Tarot deck, the card that correlates with the sign of Pisces is The Moon card. This card comes right after The Star, and right before The Sun. Both The Star and The Sun emit their own light: The Moon is only a reflector and sometimes, a distorter, an illusion-maker. How? By existing in the dark, by playing on our emotions, the tides that rise and fall within us all. The Star connotes a coming back home, an acceptance into vulnerability. Now that we've spent time healing and reconnected to our core truth, it is time to take another deep dive into the subconscious mind and emotional fields within. The Moon card imagery reflects myths, imagination, wildness, and surrealism—other than the Wheel, this is the only card in the Major Arcana that contains no human figures. The figures that are depicted are quite strange: a howling dog and a howling wolf, a crawfish or crab, half submerged in water, half in land, and an unwaveringly bright Moon. How do we reconcile our wildness? Is being tame overrated?

These dogs can symbolize different states to reckon with and pay attention to. How do we reconcile our feral, wild state with our tamed, disciplined state? The wolf is on one side of the image, the domestic dog on the either. These dogs were also sometimes called the dogs of Hecate—the Queen of the Witches, the Crone archetype, who also correlates with The High Priestess card—she who wears the Triple Goddess on her head (a.k.a. the Crown of Hathor); she who is surrounded by every ancient religion and spiritual practice there is; she who holds infinite wisdom, source energy, knowing beyond words or explanation. Both Hecate and the High Priestess are a few of the most infinitely powerful magic makers in the archetypal pantheon.

While The High Priestess usually represents a more quiet and introspective receiving of information or intuition, The Moon card speaks to a more turbulent energy. Emotions need to be drawn out and expunged. The crayfish in between two worlds can scuttle back to its natural state, or decide to take a brave new journey, crossing new thresholds, expanding beyond the known, moving through fear. The Moon card suggests utilizing the subconscious and the emotions to catapult into new zones. Sometimes it's about paying attention to your animal body, your feral emotions, dreams, messages, and getting weirder.

Do you need to do the hokey-pokey, and turn yourself around?
Can your sensitivities be a source of pride?
Do you need to buy yourself a trophy for the incredible amount of tears you've shed?

The symbol of Pisces also resembles that ancient symbol of the ouroboros—the all-knowing serpent that, like the Moon, speaks to the cyclic nature of the universe. Life out of death, the ouroboros eats its own tail to sustain its life. Ouroboros represents the hard-won renewal that can only come out of destruction; the wise serpent—in ancient times thought to encircle the Earth—the cosmic serpent encasing the World egg, or a serpent god, at times correlating with sea dragons.

The ouroboros also encapsulates the idea of darkness and light creating the whole— another yin-yang, the mystery and known, the night in the day, the day in the night— the dual nature of all things, not in conflict. The balance lies in the duality. Energy flows in a circular fashion—at times internally, and at times externally, in coexistence and the acceptance of such. Illusions give way to reality, and the allowance and inquisition of the subconscious—dreams that lay on top of the mundanity of daily life. Our flaws can coexist with our strengths. In fact, they must.

Is your process a vicious circle or an inquisitive cycle?

Where can you welcome the unknown?

How can you best embody this daily, weekly?

In ancient times, the power of fertility in plants was seen to emanate from the Moon. Traditionally, those millions of people—mostly women— who were persecuted for "witchcraft" were actually wise community herbalists, attuned to the messages of plant life and the elements. They utilized their knowledge to help those around them. The cartoonish caricature of the witch cackling around a cauldron at the Full Moon was most likely taken from women creating herbal infusions, poultices, tinctures, and other fortifying remedies. To this day, farmers and those in the agriculture industry know to work with the cycles of the Moon in planting and harvesting.

At this September Full Moon, traditionally the time of the second harvest, the suggested ritual is to create dual sunlight- and moonlight-infused flower and crystal essence formulas for you to use for your personal support. This is a way for you to infuse and ingest the darkness and the light, knowing both feed and stabilize the other.

A flower essence is the bioenergetic imprint of a flower transferred into water. Essences utilize all of the elements. Fire (the Sun), water (spring water), earth (the flower, crystal, or plant), air (the outside environment) and center (or Spirit; i.e., your intention). With this ritual, you can work through the archetypes of The Star, The Sun, and The Moon.

Depending on the weather where you are located, you will have to plan ahead to make your essences. I would recommend perhaps making your sunlight-activated flower essence a day or two before the Full Moon, maybe on that Sunday, as long as it isn't raining or cloudy. You could make your moonlight-activated essence on the night of the Full Moon, or the evening before.

Remember: intention is always more important than exact timing!

What my intentions are at this time:

Any messages from my conscious or subconscious self that is coming up for me:

What does my "dark" look like at this time:

What does my "light" look like at this time:

How can I integrate and accept these both more:

Any notes on symbology, recurring icons, or archetypes:

September Full Moon Suggested Ritual:
Sunlight & Moonlight Flower Essences

Suggested Affirmation: "My intuition and sensitivity guide me into groundedness. I give myself the support that I need and I am open to receiving support."

You will need:

Two or three 1- or 2-ounce glass dropper bottles (you can always save and sterilize tincture bottles, as I do)
Small, preferably glass, funnel
Clear glass or crystal bowl
Glass jar with lid, like a mason jar, filled with fresh spring water
Tweezers or a leaf for removing the flower from water
Brandy, 100-proof vodka, or vegetable glycerin/apple cider vinegar
Garden shears or scissors
Labels or stickers

Making the sunlight-infused flower essence:

1. Think about what you'd like emotional or behavioral support or help with at this time. What is an ongoing issue or emotional pattern you'd like to begin to unravel and move through? What external habits or consciousness would you like some support with shifting? Brainstorm some ideas, no matter how specific or vague.

2. Spend some time in the outdoors. Your favorite hiking trail, meadow, and national park are all good. If you live in a very urban environment, go to the closest park. Notice what wildlife you are

drawn to, what flowers seem to speak to you. Why? Can you describe what about them attracts you? What adjectives do you come up with for the flower? Can you spend some time with them, listening to them? Can you identity what flower they are?

3. Identify your flower. Figure out what the flower is that you will be working with. Determine that it is not poisonous or potentially allergy-inducing. You might have to do some research. When in doubt, **do not use** a plant or flower you are unfamiliar with or cannot identify! Think about key components of your flower: for example, dandelion flowers might be about spreading out and taking up space, as their seeds become mini-helicopters, traveling far distances to propagate! Commune with your flower and figure out what it can help you with.

4. Ask the plant's permission and gather your flowers. You don't need any more than 2 – 3 mature flowers. Ask the plant for permission and thank it. Take care to try to not touch the flower; you can use tweezers, or leaves. Some people like to leave an offering for the plant: pour some water into the earth it grows from.

5. Create your essence. The suggested place is in the environment the flower comes from if it is an undisturbed and calm place. Place your bowl on a flat surface outside, in a place that will be exposed to direct sunlight. The more direct sunlight, the better. Pour the water into your bowl. Then, using tweezers, or a twig or leaf, place the flowers face-up in the water. They do not need to be submerged at all. Let the water sit for 2 – 4 hours. Some people like to pray, meditate, sing, journal, or do other ceremony while this is happening.

6. Remove the flowers from the bowl. If you are in the environment from where you gathered the flower, you can return the flower back to its origin. Using the funnel, pour the water into your mason jar until it is half full. Then, add your preservative to the other half (brandy, vodka, apple cider vinegar, or vegetable glycerin.

7. Congratulations! You've made a flower essence! This is your "mother essence." Label this with the flower, day, Moon phase, and any other information you would like.

8. Take 10 – 30 drops from the "mother essence" and put in a 1 – 2-ounce dropper bottle. Fill that dropper bottle with your preserving agent. Label your bottle, and take 3 – 30 drops, 3 – 5 times a day, as needed.

Making the moonlight-infused crystal essence:

1. Think about what you'd like spiritual support or help with at this time. What is an ongoing issue or emotional pattern you'd like to begin to unravel and move through? This can be subtle. Brainstorm some ideas, no matter how specific or vague.

2. Spend some time with your crystal collection. Meditate with some of your favorites, or put them all on a tabletop and close your eyes. Let your hands pass over them until you feel drawn to one, two, or three of them.

3. If you don't know much about this crystal, do some research. Does this crystal contain metals or other toxins that are not safe for ingesting? Do not use a crystal or stone you are not sure about! Was it used for ancient rites and ceremo-

ny? As a protective amulet? Or as make-up or paint? Figure out what the crystals can help you with. Meditate again with them and pay attention to any downloads you get. Remember to do due diligence and confirm your crystal is safe to submerge in water and ingest: many are not! Safe crystals to use are rose quartz, clear quartz, and amethyst.

4. Cleanse your chosen crystals. You can do this with saltwater in a glass bowl for up to 24 hours. You can do this with dry salt as well, covering your crystals with salt. Running water, such as in a stream bed, also works. After the dry or wet salt bath, you can run them under cold water to rinse any salt particles off.

5. Charge and program your crystals. In a calm, quiet space, bring your intentions to the forefront of your mind. Connect with each crystal, and put your focused intention into each one. You may speak this, chant this, or sing this while holding the crystal or putting your hand over it. Sometimes people like passing this over a lit, corresponding candle.

6. Create your moonlight crystal essence. After the sun has set, bring your bowl, water, and chosen clean crystals outside into a safe, calm, undisturbed space. You may also wish to bring additional herbs to place around your bowl for additional vibrational support (i.e., fresh rosemary, lavender). Place the crystals in the bowl, and pour spring water over them. You may wish to draw down the Moon, say a prayer, sing a song, or any other ritual. Leave the bowl outside in the moonlight for at least 2 hours.

Now you have two different infused essences: one activated by sunlight, the other by moonlight! You may take separately, or mix the two together.

What I worked on around this time:

What my feelings were at this time:

Other notes:

SEPTEMBER 12th: LAST QUARTER MOON in GEMINI 11:25 PM PST, 11:53 PM MOONRISE PST

Outmoded Ideas of the Self: Changing Your Mind

"If you change your mind, I'm the first in line
Honey, I'm still free, take a chance on me
If you need me, let me know, gonna be around
If you got no place to go when you're feeling down
If you're all alone when the pretty birds have flown,
Honey, I'm still free, take a chance on me
Gonna do my very best and it ain't no lie
If you put me to the test, if you let me try"
—ABBA

Our Last Quarter Moon, the only one of September, arrives today, Tuesday, September 12th. The Moon, if visible to your naked eye in the evening sky, should appear about half lit up, the light coming from the left side. The Full Moon of the month was one week ago. If any messages came through, now might feel like the natural time to distill them, write them down, work with them. If any huge emotions came up for your sweet self during the Full Moon on the 6th or around that time, it might be time to analyze them, parse them out, look for patterns that can aid you moving forward. After today the light ebbs off the Moon as it orbits counterclockwise away from us, closer to the Sun. We are a little over one week away from the next New Moon.

The Major Arcana card in the Tarot that corresponds with Gemini is The Lovers. On one level this card is about love, desire, and cosmic unity—sometimes with another, but truly it is with self, the merging of dualities or disparate facets of the self on the inside. Close your eyes. Do you see anything? Is there a universe inside of this body you inhabit? What does it feel like, look like, what images or messages pop into your head? Is it yours and yours alone, or is it meant to be shared—each interior speck of stardust a flashlight for the other lovers, each secret a new song to be belted out in front of an audience? Right now in your life, what is on the inside that needs to come out and where is it time to process certain external situations on the inside?

The Lovers card, to me, is also about choice and life's path. About what happens, what decisions get made, what actions activated, after being presented with the truth. In the traditional deck, behind the man is the Tree of Life, behind the woman is the Tree of Knowledge. A loaded message, or temptation, delivered by the slithering serpent, that maligned archetype of dangerous influence.

Consider the snake, shedding its skin. The average snake sheds its skin two to four times a year. Serpents' skins don't grow with them, like other animals' skins do. They cast off their exterior periodically to allow for growth and to remove parasites that might have attached themselves.

When we are working with magick and manifestation, we must take a holistic approach and examine our blocks and fears, the scarcities that circle back around, that craggy claw pressing the tops of our panic buttons in the middle of the night. Some of these patterns are old identities we've clung to that have been programmed into us so long ago we might not have even been aware they were forming; some have been programmed even before we were born! To step forward into the new, to conjure up healthier ways, sustenance, and sustainability, requires bidding farewell to old identities—and with them, the parasites of bogged-down thought forms, limiting self-talk, and the stagnation that accompanies them.

At this time, think about and examine any conscious or unconscious ideas around your own identity, personality traits, or behavior that might have be stopping you from working your best magick. You might ask yourself where this narrative is coming from. Is it even true? Did anyone ever even say it out loud to you?

Maybe you are afraid to say goodbye to your role as the "fuck-up" in the family so you keep your dreams of going back to business school on the back burner. Maybe your idea of yourself as the "responsible, professional one" stops you from taking on a career that is harder to define. While these examples are very surface-oriented, your patterns and limitations can get much deeper, embedded in your bones. A concretized fear of abandonment results in the inability to form intimate and vulnerable connections. Webs woven out of barbed wire around our brains tell us that we don't deserve safety or recognition, so we stay in our identities as the wallflower, supporting others who might be selfish, or volatile, or abusive. We've all got our own ingrained stories, we all have identities, ideas, and patterns that we must sacrifice in order to make way for lives that are in alignment with our true, helpful spirits and our beautiful, expansive selves.

We must transmute fear into love.

You might ask yourself where this narrative is coming from in your body. Sitting quietly, you can state this belief. Is there a correlation to a body part? If your throat clogs up or clenches up, this might have to do with not feeling safe speaking up. Practice clearly communicating your truth. If it is lodged deep in your tummy or gut, check in with your feelings around personal power. Do more investigating about what has corded to you energetically, where it lies, and what the sources are.

Consider the snake, shedding its skin: its dead, disintegrated cells from a past self, unrecognizable. All in the name of growing, getting larger and stronger.

There must always be a period of communicating change when we are attempting to make long-lasting improvements in our lives. Telling our deep, subconscious mind we will no longer treat ourself in a certain, harmful way. Telling people they can no longer treat us in disrespectful fashions. Saying no to certain job offers, because they do not feel aligned with where we are currently. Sometimes, when we are in a period of dismantling, a lot of old temptations will pop up in our lives. An old flame appears after we've vowed to be single for a period and work on ourselves. A big part of the process is floating in the unknown, breathing and remaining calm, doing the work, and staying in faith and trust. Some people are terrified of the in-between, of going through the emptiness before the shift, and so they stay, locked in familiar patterns. At this time, examine what scares you about making changes. Where have you gotten too cozy?

Similarly, when we do banishing or releasing spell work, we must be prepared through and through for the consequences of such. Once I did a "banish bad debt" spell. At the time of the spell, I was very focused on my "debt" as being a large amount of student loans. Within a week, I got a large bill from the city's tax office I never knew I owed, as well as an email from an emotionally manipulative person from my past, stating I somehow owed them money for something from ages ago. I knew immediately the spell was working, albeit with some unintended and unknown "bad debt" to be dealt with. Because what's the worst kind of "bad debt"? Debt you either didn't know you owed, or didn't really owe at all! The first step was clearing all that up, and out. At this time, is there clearing and unclogging work that needs to be attended to, either spell-wise, or energetically?

Are you ready to work through uncomfortable feelings and no longer block your own paths to change?

During the Balsamic period of this September, a week before the New Moon, what old cells are going to be sloughed off? What useless titles, adjectives are you no longer willing to put up with? Are you ready to be in the void? Are you ready to say goodbye, once and for all, to situations not in alignment with your dreams and goals?

What is draining your focus?

Your mental energy?

Where are you scattered?

Where are you bored, and what needs spicing up?

Are you ready to make new choices?

What stories about yourself are you ready to stop telling, once and for all?

Helpful herbs for release and support through change: Dandelion root, lemon balm, pink yarrow
Helpful crystals through change: Crocodile jasper, any stones in the jasper family, kyanite, ruby fuchsite, obsidian, jet
Tarot cards to meditate on: The Lovers, Death, 9 of Swords, 8 of Cups
Other notes on progress and process at this time:

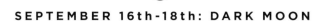

Reconnecting with Rest

We all need to rest.
We all need to slow down.
We all need to just do one thing, and only one thing, at a time.
We all need to stare at the wall, trace the carpet, breathe in deep, inhale the fumes of our miso soup. Sip tea loudly alone, close our eyes in the middle of the day. Count our breaths per minute, slow down our inhales.

We all need to stretch, stare at our pores in the mirror, hum an unknown song and arch our toes, quietly clip our toenails while sitting on the toilet seat, shove our fingers slowly through the water in a bath, fish a cool cucumber slice out of the fridge and hold against our eyelids. We need to hold hands quietly with a friend or lover, stroke our pet's paw.

To think about snails, sloths, water carving out rocks over the ages.

According to journalist Lisa Eadicicco, people in the United States across all age groups check their phones 46 times per day for an average of 4.5 hours daily of waking life. ("Americans Check Their Phones 8 Billion Times a Day," Dec 15, 2015) Our eyes are fatigued; our brains need to rest. We need time to process. Studies have shown that when we try to multi-task, the stress hormone cortisol and adrenaline are produced, which can ultimately lead to brain fogginess and confusion. (*The Organized Mind*, Daniel J. Levitin, page 96.) It is important to slow down and do one thing at a time.

Capitalism wants to send us our validation only in the form of our productivity. What we are doing, who we know, how much we are making, what we own. We aren't worthwhile unless the to-do list has been checked off, the form has been sent back, every minute in our lives has been accounted for in our résumés. In the scope and timeline of the collective, this is all quite new.

Who are we, really, when not trying to land the next deal, plan the next photoshoot and marketing campaign, sprint towards our next goal, prove something, push to outdo ourselves? Resting allows us to touch base with our essence. To sink softly into sensation, not relying on outcome. We turn our attention inward, connecting with our core self and all the variations of that self via dreams, emotions, body pain or stiffness, looping narratives, and positive or negative self-talk. Sit with those quietly, and breathe through them.

Resting is important because it reinforces our self-love. Resting tells us that we are okay and deserve a break no matter what we've done, or haven't done.

Practicing resting and mindfulness is important because we can take these qualities into our daily life. We can complete tasks with calmness, one at a time. We can pause before reacting, or catch ourselves before spiraling out more quickly.

Oftentimes, when we go quickly, we contract. Think about the state of your body on a daily basis. Are you tense? Running around? Jaw clenched? True rest and relaxation helps us soften.

Creatively, resting and engaging in other activities besides work is important because it stimulates the muse. Personally, I get the majority of my creative messages and inspiration when I am meditating, practicing breathwork, running, or in the shower. If I didn't do all these activities you would not be holding this book!

Magically, resting is important because it allows us to reconnect to the self and a reset back into the present moment. If the present moment is calm, content, and intentional, then that is the plane we are vibrating at. When we are frazzled, frenetic, jacked up on stress, giving our power away to emails, phones, or the endlessness of our to-do lists, then we are only perpetuating more of that in our lives. We aren't actively manifesting anything we put forth in our spell work—particularly if what we are precisely trying to attract is calmness, joyfulness, or peace!

When we consciously rest, when we lay down, close our eyes, and only focus on our breath and our heartbeat, we reconnect with Source and Spirit. As we notice our heartbeat, we conjure a sense of wonder. How remarkable that we are alive! What is making our heart beat? Life force, vitality, energy. What is behind the heartbeat? The same thing that is behind all the other heartbeats on this planet. This is what we all have in common.

At this Dark Moon time, put rest and relaxation front and center.

How do I feel about resting or slowing down?

Am I trying to do too much?

What I can consciously do to slow down at the end of this cycle:

What that will look like:

SEPTEMBER 19th: NEW MOON in VIRGO 10:30 PM PST, 6:01 AM MOONRISE PST

Connecting with the Holistic Body

by Esmé Weijun Wang

The New Moon is my favorite phase of the lunar cycle. Though the moon is, at this time, not visible to us, the heavenward darkness that occurs creates a blank slate for Virgo wishes and intentions. The sign of Virgo, though commonly understood as tied to Type-A personalities and a desire for structure and organization, is also linked to healing and healers. In particular, those of us dealing with chronic health issues—or who simply wish to bring a greater sense of ease to our relationships with our bodies—are well-matched to this New Moon.

Having dealt with chronic mental illness since I was eleven years old, as well as disabling and chronic physical illness since my late 20s, I respectfully approach this New Moon in Virgo by using divination to obtain guidance regarding thorny questions of wellness, and how to move forward with my relationship to wellness and healing.

For this, I recommend using your favorite Tarot deck. Prepare your space by creating quiet; cleanse the area with whichever method you favor (I tend to like palo santo, but your mileage may vary). Prepare your body by drinking a large glass of water—you may be tempted to skip this step, but the glass of water is non-negotiable unless you have a physical condition that prohibits it. I also recommend lighting a candle.

Draw a card for each of the following questions:

- What is the state of my body now?
- What is the state of my mind now?
- What is my holistic self yearning for?
- What is the first step I must take to nourish my holistic self?
- What have I been ignoring when it comes to my well-being?

Take out your journal. Jot down your intuitive interpretations for each question and its corresponding card. If you would like more information, or if a card is confusing, draw another card to gain further clarity.

You may, in this process of drawing cards and journaling, find that you wish to ask additional questions about wellness, nourishment, and your holistic self. Freely ask those additional questions and make as many notes as you wish.

After you have exhausted all possible avenues for further question-and-answer, consider an intention to set during this Virgo New Moon.

Ideas for possible intention-setting include:

I call more _____ into my life.
I would like to feel _____ , and will take actions toward doing so.

My body desires _____, and I will provide more of _____ over this lunar cycle.

As you set your intention for this lunar cycle, allow yourself to fully feel your way into the bodily sensations of what might happen if you do, indeed, bring this intention to fruition. Take several minutes of sitting in silence. Allow the felt sense to carry you.

Speak your intention aloud and thank the higher source that has carried you through life to this point before extinguishing your candle.

Drink another glass of water.

You are complete.

Additional journal prompts:

What lessons has your body taught you during your lifetime?

How easy is it for you to listen to the messages of your body?

Are you afraid of your body, and why?

Do you believe that illness is a punishment of some sort?

What would it look like for you to heal in mind, body, and spirit?

What is the most nourishing thing you could do for your body right now? This week? During this lunar cycle?

Suggested Affirmation: "I am complete as I am."

Assess and Reset

This Wednesday, September 27th, is the first quarter Moon. Our New Moon was a week ago, our Full Moon eight days away. The Autumn Equinox was five days ago; the light is shifting. Some of it is still left at the end of our work day. It's almost the end of the month; we're sliding into the last third of this year. The hourglass is half full, the sand moving up—for the moment. Energy may feel high; our capacity to do more work could be wider and deeper.

The Last Quarter Moon this month asked us to shed ideas about identity and perceived notions of self. The New Moon was about wellness and healing. At this time, examine your ideas for personal important goals and ambitions and what needs to happen. Assess and reset what your consistent actions will be at this time: clear, carved out, yours and yours alone.

Mentally, energetically, and emotionally take stock. Where are you ready to go beyond? Jump over, crawl under? There's a correlation between the sign of Capricorn and work. Here we are, in September. Summer is over, the school year is well underway. What do you want to accomplish in the next week, the next month?

Be clear, concise, determined.

A lot of times our spell work and intention settings do not work as well they could because we are afraid to ask for exactly what we want. A lot of times our relationships aren't as authentic as we'd like them to be because we do not communicate what we really need. Time and time again I've had students in workshops who admit they don't do spell work based upon their deep desires because it isn't truly "for the greater good." Gentle reader, the ancient French root of the word "desire" is from the phrase *de sidere*, which means "from the stars." Your desires are greater than you, summoned from the cosmos.

If it is what you truly want, harms no one, and will make you happy, then it is for the greater good. We can't feed others unless we are fed. We can't help others, teach, give our time freely, if we are overly wanting. Casting spells for wealth, better health, or more recognition is not wrong or overly selfish. We must put the mask on ourselves first, before we help others on the plane careening through the sky. Of course, excessively using "self-care" for excuses, or refusing to help others in need, is not useful.

(At times, incessant themes around spell work or desires can point to certain areas where the quality needs to be given more freely to oneself. Greed for greed's sake is a downward spiral. A much too scratchy itch for fame and recognition points to an endless hole inside, one that can never be filled no matter how many screaming fans one has. Just a note, sweetest heart, to be very clear about why you want what you want, and to seek out simple ways to give these baseline needs to *yourself* first before knocking on any other doors to get them.)

At this time, I encourage you to write down a few wishes or goals that make you feel selfish, uncouth, or even frivolous. Only you know what will give you contentment and pleasure. Could you cast a spell around these desires during the next week, the upcoming Waxing Moon phase?

You could also reexamine goals or ambitions and fine tune them to get them more in line with your true self, the soul's deep wishes. A lot of what we really want out of our lives is less about things, and more about moments. Less about status, and more about connecting with others. More about fine-tuning our inherent talents and interests to their most mastered state, and less about endlessly chasing carrots on sticks put in front of us by society.

When we think about working outside of the dominant cultures' egocentric capitalism and the crippling structures of rich/poor, success/failure based upon money, ego, and other strange forms of status, we allow a freedom that can loosen our fears, anxieties, and blocks. When our success is defined by how we want to feel, who we wish to include, who and what we know we must protect, what we must honor, what we desire to create, and what value systems we dedicate our goals to, there's no way we can fail. When our soul's bedrock and baselines are crystal quartz clear, it is all in our hands already, raised in reverence, wrapped in respect for our dedication and the devoted pathways of our pursuits.

Who are you working for?

Why?

How?

It is now time to begin. To walk the walk. For real. With manifestation work and goal setting, at a certain point the action items must get crossed off. Get started, whether in a tiny teacup way, or bolder and larger than you've tried to before. Gulp hard, past the frogs in your throat, and move forward in tangible ways this week. Enact some of the things that precisely scare you the most.

Starting sloppy and unsure is better than not starting at all. Putting one foot in front of the other, over and over, when in alignment with one's clear goals, is sometimes the only thing to do.

We have to commit to making changes before they occur.

What next?

What moves do you need to make? What spells would help you with this?

Here's the thing: magick works best when you do.
You are magick, through and through.
Work your magick this week: build altars to your ambitions, then bring that ambition out into the world.

So mote it be!

Ask yourself: How will this week be different?
How can I make this day different, more in alignment with my goals?
Is it simply giving yourself more time? Breathing? Carving out space for joy?
Do you to wake up ten minutes earlier to meditate, jog, journal, or breathe?

Suggested Activities:

This week, clarify your action steps around your goals. Be specific, clear, and committed. If you need an accountability friend, then get one. Maybe they need one too!

Get a book that is a biography of someone you look up to in your desired or current field. Make notes in the book, or copy quotes from the author to inspire you.

Finish one or two annoying tasks that you've been making excuses around not completing or starting.

Build an altar to your project, goals, or ambitions. Visit it every day this week.

If you are casting a spell to build a practice, project, or business, cast a specific spell around the smooth, useful, profitable, and focused "doing" of the thing. Infuse the "work" part of it with magic. Then, when you begin to work on it, light the candle and bring the talisman into your work space. Take moments before you begin to work to connect with your higher self, with the magic you felt during your spell. Know that your work is blessed and the benefits to you and others reverberate outward.

Helpful crystals for drive and determination: Carnelian, Tiger's eye, pyrite, picture jasper, bloodstone
Helpful herbs/tinctures for strength and energy: Nettles, bamboo, cinnamon, hawthorn, burdock, cinnamon

Notes on this month:

Intentions for the next:

OCTOBER 2017

OCTOBER 5th: FULL MOON
OCTOBER 12th: LAST QUARTER
OCTOBER 19th: NEW MOON
OCTOBER 27th: FIRST QUARTER

October is pumpkins and cauldrons, dark maroon dreams unfolding into the blackest black evening. October is beautifully dead leaves crunching under our feet. October is what I've referred to as a "bridge month"—between the sun of summer and the dark of winter we stretch a bit, perhaps to tie these two dichotomies together. The month of marigolds and ghosts and colder nights. This month, most birds have flown south.

This is the season of the thinning veil. In ancient times people believed the Goddess wore a veil—if you could see underneath it, you could see into the future. Widows frequently wore veils, as did brides: to keep both vulnerable parties protected. While this use is synonymous with protection, to pull back the veil is to reveal the truth. With Halloween, Samhain, and Day of the Dead exclamation marks at the end of the month, this is certainly the time to examine our own truisms. We can look to the past to excavate both pain and enlightenment.

Where are we held captive by narratives from the past?

What are our new truths?

This is certainly the time to honor our ancestors, honor our past lives, be aware of messages of all kinds. To reacquaint ourselves to seeing in the dark again. To reconnect with fortitude, with our own creative energies, as well as the fight for others and *all* our futures.

The artist Kerry James Marshall, born this month, said: "I think we need to remember…that a lot of energy was put into changing things to get us to the point where we are now. But being where we are now doesn't mean that we don't have to put in the same kind of energy to get us to a place where we ought to be."

The suggested activities around the Moons this month have to do with honoring our ancestors, thinking about our periods and release, joining together with community to share blessings, and creating charms to act as talismans for our manifestations or psychic protection. This month, reflect on your lineage and legacy. Join together through all the change to create more joyful and holistic structures for all.

October Astro Roll Call
By Diego Basdeo

A brief snapshot of the stars for your monthly needs by your one and only lunar dude, Diego Basdeo. For more information on how the planets are working with the Moon go to diegobasdeo.com and check out Lunations, a moon-focused astrological forecast.

Aries: The energy of Aries pairs well with the New Moon. I don't mean wine and cheese. I mean like Sade and sex. Like war and steel. Like punk and aggression. Be explosive walking into this spooky month and bring excitement and new new into your relationships.

Taurus: Exiting somewhere is always an entrance to some other place. Make an entrance, babe. Understand the innocence of trying. Let yourself try something new without judgment. It's good for your health.

Gemini: A higher calling is knocking and it can be influencing your life for better or for worse right now. Chances are, it's been hanging out with you for a while now. I think there is a greater understanding of being at one with the world now, however troubled or peaceful. Respond in kind with demonstrations of twinship with every person out here. Play, and trust the truth that comes through.

Cancer: It's about street cred this go round. Whether you're a soft shell or solid all the way through, it's time to get some exposure. Put up a new insta vid with you moving to your fave song. Hook up three people with your connections. Give people a reason to love you and I bet they will. I mean, look at you. You're gorgeous. Use your swagger this month to warm the home as well.

Leo: The moons and planets are working for a greater understanding. Take a look at your dogmas, dude. Think about what you are most principled about. There's a chance that the people in your milieu may need to diversify a lil bit. Bring in a voice you don't hear too much to collect info or ways of thinking you might not have considered.

Virgo: You might find yourself in a hall of mirrors this month. You may want to shut shit down, but that isn't advisable. The storm will pass and you will have an opportunity to see where you get undone. The later half of the month can be a great time to find people who can help you with those problem areas.

Libra: For your birthday, put out water for your house guests, bring in fresh flowers, and enjoy your things, your people, the stuff that you let grace your skin and heart regularly. What a precious gift it is to be able to enjoy a thing, to feel another living thing touch us, speak to us, and understand. Experience the "I" and then experience the "WE." Care for your life similarly. Set out water for your thoughts. Give simple gifts to let you know you care about yourself.

Scorpio: You may have to step into a role of leadership in order to be of service. Regardless of how it looks, you may be taking on a lot of responsibilities that you have the energy to accomplish now. Please make decisions that are kind to future you.

Sagittarius: Plan a really fantastic date. Let the date be a showcase of all your creative power. Let it perform your strengths, your visions, and your desires of how life should be. You don't need to spend a lot of money to experience extravagance and pleasure. Your strengths will be needed later in the month. Practice organizing around what brings joy.

Capricorn: You can't learn others' lessons. You CAN offer your skills to others so that they may have tools to take on their challenges. With patient communication, you can ease the burden you put on yourself to take care of others so much. Partnership in work can be a wonderful thing and bringing your strength of skill sharing can help keep healthy boundaries and strengthen the work you do.

Aquarius: This is a fantastic time to be about you. Get out there and tell the people that you have brilliant ideas, fascinations, and inquiries to discuss. The cue for a more internal and studious discourse is when it comes to your opinion of fairness. While the drive to talk about values may be pressing, you want to be careful not to move into a position of argument. Expansiveness is the name of the game.

Pisces: This is a great month to balance the books. Money is a means to an end. What is your "end"? How is it in service to what you believe in? It can bring up challenges around being assertive with your ways of making money. You might have a unique view on the inner workings of how financial capital works but you might be afraid to take advantage of it.

Our Stories, Our Selves

"…As long as you remember what you have seen, then nothing is gone. As long as you remember, it is part of this story we have together." — Leslie Marmon Silko, *Ceremony*

On Thursday, October 5th, we begin the month with the Full Moon, known in October as the Blood Moon. This Moon is also called the Hunter's Moon and the Shedding Moon. (This year it is also technically the Harvest Moon, as it falls closest to the Autumn Equinox that happened last month on the 22nd.) The Sun is in Libra, the month is five days old; it's time to begin with gratitude for apples, gratitude for falling leaves, for goofy Halloween movies, for old friends and new ones. Appreciation for making it through these nine months of the year so far, of sticking to some things and leaving behind others, and remembering to drink water and take deep breaths, and the appreciation that you've shown yourself. You love yourself by releasing the grip of perfection and criticism. Speaking to yourself a bit more sweetly, or lavishing praise on yourself for doing the dishes or smiling at a stranger, or stepping into your power more, or taking naps more, or standing in the moonlight more. Or if you haven't yet done any of these this is a reminder that we've got a Full Moon today, and if nothing else, you can stand under her reflected light for five minutes, put your crystals out, take a bath, write in your journal, smile to yourself, start where you are, talk to your cat, or your plants or your face in the mirror. Speak out loud who you are and what you want and what is coming to you!

October is the month that Samhain falls in—some witches' New Year. For many Pagans and practitioners, the Wheel of the Year begins later this month, at Samhain. This month marks the end of the harvest and the descent into darkness. Before there was light, there was darkness. We can step into this darkness, and work with its gifts. At this time, this month, it is believed that the veil between living and dead is the thinnest. This is the time to remember, to memorialize, and reflect on who helped make us who we are—and thank them. To honor and respect those who have shaped our thinking, our behavior, those who are in some part responsible for our facial features, our blood types, how many eyelashes frame our eyelids.

Some of us have more complicated and ambivalent relationships with our family tree. Learn more information; there may be contextualization about your own patterns there. Maybe a lineage of abuse and addiction can clarify some of your behaviors. Look for insights and knowledge. Send a smidge (or more) of some rose quartz love and compassion to those in your family tree who had some kind of Big Hurt they were dealing with. Sadly, much of it did not have to do with you, and sadly, you were affected by it. Examine the knowing that resides in your bones, the inkiest, shiniest piece of smoky quartz.

For those of us whose family is chosen, we can always take time to honor and celebrate them, whether those souls are living or passed on. Our ancestors could be people we've read, listened to: those who have touched us deeply though we've never met them, or influential teachers or notable protagonists of our profession.

For those of us whose stories have traditionally been silenced by others, silenced by our own sacrifices, or stolen, it is imperative that we speak and share them.

Witches believe that one of our many responsibilities in our lifetime is to work on healing ancestral wounds. We can work on forgiving and acknowledging ancestors who have passed on, as well as ancestors we have never met. Through this, we have not only the ability to work towards healing our lineage, but also healing future descendants—whether they are related to us via blood or not. We work towards healing our past and our future through the work we do in the present. There is always now, and now is always changing based upon our inner and outer work and actions. To make amends with the past is to send good luck into the future.

During this Full Moon, reflect on the different parts of your identity, those inherently "you" and those that have been nurtured through others. Are there any that came from someone else in some way? To honor your ancestors, your lineage, your family, or your chosen family is to honor yourself, as well as place yourself in the web of the collective. Write down any stories about your family. Write down any poignant memories of people who influenced you deeply. Write a story about your life, one you'd like to be known for and remembered. Think about ways, moving forward, to befriend elders, or nurture the relationships you have with the elders in your life.

Dear heart, it is time to tell your story: to bring forth, in ceremony, with awareness of where you came from, and how that background, in part, makes you who you are. If it is time to write your memoir, write it. No one else will. If it is time to learn the language of your ancestors, begin. If it is time to do research on your background, ask questions of the elders in your family or community, begin this process. Take a DNA test, research the traditions of your blood and bones. On this Blood Moon, start harvesting in a tangible way. One day it might be time to pass on this knowledge. For some of us, that one day is now.

We've been trained to keep our stories to ourselves—particularly if shameful, and shameful, in this culture, certainly does cover a lot of ground and many fuzzy definitions. We have all seen the heartbreak of hiding, covering up, survivor blaming, and gaslighting: in our school systems, some of us didn't learn about internment camps, the accurate history of slavery in this country, or the genocide against Native Americans in North America. If we are women, shame has been thrown at us by trying to make us feel uneasy with our bodies, or for covering up too much, not covering up enough, our periods if we get them, hair, appearance, and other markers of the patriarchal paradigms' idea of "femininity". If we are gender non-conforming or trans, the shame thrown at us can be around our identities, bodies, and freedom. So many attempts of dehumanizing us; the shame that cloaks abuse, that shame that tries to keep us all quiet.

It is time to take back what is ours, to no longer feel ashamed of speaking up. Indeed, we are in a time where our shared stories are saving us, serving as lighthouses and motivation.

Is it a herstory? Is it a theystory? A zestory? Sure! This is also ourstory. In recounting and telling, we share. We become a resource, a familiar sigh of relief, a reminder we are not alone.

In telling our stories, in framing and contextualizing our own narrative, we are asserting our choice. Our autonomy via the voice. Our knowledge. We need every remembering. Every last one. We need to encourage the telling of other people's stories—particularly those who are historically marginalized—through asking our loved ones about their life, through listening compassionately, through sharing and talking in groups, buying books and zines about people's stories, recounting the contributions of others, signal boosting others' accomplishments, and educating each other as much as possible.

The following suggested ritual to honor the Full Moon is by building an altar to meaningful ancestors. You may feel called to honor some. With that comes offerings, prayer, gratitude, and the promise that you will continue to remember, and continue to pass on the gifts that they have given you.

With some, you may be called to forgive. To make amends, to attempt to let go of some of the hurtful patterns or imprints that have been passed down to you. To understand that in doing so, the load lessens psychically, emotionally, mentally for you, for your community, for your future self. For people you haven't met yet, as well as their children and community members.

And lastly, during this Full Moon, attend to yourself. Your present and future self. Your stories. The ones that are yours and yours alone. Commit to telling them, to sharing them, in a way that feels accurate and authentic. Whether it is a dance, a zine, a class, a garden, an archive, or something else entirely, make a promise to follow through. Do it for your chosen family, for the greater collective. Do it for you. Do it for the healing that blossoms open our heart when our stories are listened to and our unique gifts are truly seen. That is a great offering for us, a true promise to humanity. After we've exhaled our last exhale, when our bones are dust and ash, our stories and our sharing are what remain.

As the witch adage says: "What is remembered lives!"

What stories is it time for me to share?

How will I do this?

What needs to be exorcised out of my life at this time? How will I do this?

Who do I need to forgive at this time? How can I do this?

What are some promises I'm making to myself in service of my authentic voice, my unique stories?

Where will I no longer let shame or fear hold me back?

What could come of this, if my behaviors were led by love?

Spell for the October Full Moon: Ourselves and Our Ancestors*

Suggested Affirmation: "At this time, I begin to release all the shame that has stopped me. I forgive myself and my ancestors. I embody the wisdom of my lineage. I tell my story so that others may tell theirs. I mine my one true life for its riches, I express my authentic self. This is a gift to the collective, a future healing."

Before beginning this spell, get clear about what shame or fear has stopped you. What needs to be released? Where is your lineage and your ancestors/chosen ancestors/chosen collective connected? Do you need to forgive anyone in your family, in your past, even your own past self, your own past lives? (This correlates to Candle 1.)

Before beginning this spell, be clear about who and what you want to express gratitude for. This can be chosen family, friends, or those in your specific family tree. What can their lives tell you about your own? Where would you like to research folk tales, traditions, and more knowledge from your specific blood background, or chosen family background? What messages would you like more of from your chosen collective or family tree? (This correlates to Candle 2.)

Before beginning this spell, examine what specific, authentic gifts and messages you are here to impart on the planet. Be clear about what part of your story you are wanting to bring forth. If you do not yet know exactly what this is, it is okay to start with an idea, a feeling, or a couple of key words of what those are. This is what you know to be true, beyond language: a knowing you have in the depths of your bones, all the way up to the crown of your head. (This correlates to Candle 3.)

You will need:

1 candle in a glass votive for anything you wish to release at this time (suggested colors: black, purple)
1 candle in a glass votive for a connection/gratitude/offering with ancestors (suggested colors: brown, blue, indigo)
1 candle in a glass votive for connection to yourself, your stories, your gifts to the world (suggested colors: your favorite, pink, red, white, or silver)
A bowl, glass or metal for burning things in, paper, pen, matches

You may wish to include a bit of salt and/or herbs to smother your paper with after you have burned it, for purification. You may also want to anoint each candle with specific oils, or charge them with specific bits of herbs or small crystals and other small talismans.

Begin by decorating your altar around each theme/candle. You may wish to put photos of your ancestors, yourself, your dreams up as a backdrop. You may wish to include offerings, such as flowers, nuts, candy, fruit, favorite meals of people who have passed on, items that you own that belonged to them, or items that symbolize what you are ready to let go of, that you will discard after the ritual work. Consider integrating the elements of water, fire, earth, and air.

Cleanse yourself, get comfortable, cast your circle, do whatever you usually do in ritual.
If called to, anoint your candles with herbs, oil, and/or crystals.

On a piece of paper, write down what you are releasing/forgiving yourself/forgiving your ancestors for.
Read this out loud.
Put it into your bowl and burn it.
As it burns, feel tension leaving your body. Forgive any ancestors you need to. Send them love.
Imagine a place of peace for yourself and those you are connected to by blood or choice.
After the paper has been burned, you may wish to cover it with some salt and/or herbs.
Place the ashes in the first candle. Light the candle. Stare into the flame. As you concentrate on it, imagine what you are releasing getting purified and tempered by the fire.
Spend as much time as you need here, energetically, mentally, emotionally.

On a new piece of paper, write down what you are giving gratitude/thanks for. If this relationship with self and/or ancestors/chosen family is positive, you can also ask for continued connection and guidance.
Read this out loud.
Put it into your bowl and burn it.
As it burns, feel a warmth and gratitude filling up your cells. Feel your heart get warmer. Deepen your breathing, letting it expand your heart and lungs. Know that you can access this feeling at any time; you have the power of yourself and your chosen family/ancestors. Thank them/yourself, have gratitude for this, commit to showing this gratitude in the days and years following.
After the paper has been burned, you may wish to cover it with some salt and/or herbs.
Place the ashes in the second candle. Light the candle. Stare into the flame. As you concentrate on it, imagine your gratitude and thanks reverberating into your cells, your blood, the atmosphere. Know the flame continues to burn.
You may wish to state your offering. Remember or speak about what you appreciate and love about who you are making the offering to (even if it is you!).
Spend as much time as you need here, energetically, mentally, emotionally.

On another piece of paper, write down what you will be manifesting/sharing of yourself moving forward. You may wish to ask for help with this, or with a positive outcome with this. This is your wish and commitment to yourself, moving forward.
Read this out loud.
Put it into your bowl and burn it.
After the paper has been burned, you may wish to cover it with some salt and/or herbs.
Place the ashes in the third candle. Light the candle. Stare into the flame. As you concentrate on it, visualize yourself actualizing the wish, the outcome becoming real. Know that the flame is transforming your intention and thought forms into reality. As you continue to bring this about in reality, the momentum will only grow and flicker.
Spend as much time as you need here, energetically, mentally, emotionally.

Close your circle.

Keep the candles burning as long as you are home to watch them. This might last anywhere from 3-7 days. When the candles have all been burned down, pour some salt on them. Dispose of them in a trash can far outside your house. If there are items you wish to sacrifice/get rid of, do this also far from your house.
If the offerings are recyclable, put them in your compost and/or leave them outside for animals (if they are nuts or seeds).
Tidy your altar. Wipe the slate clean. In the coming week and months, be open and notice any messages or changes brought about as a result of this spell.

*The burning of the paper and placing the ashes in candles part of this ritual was introduced to me by my wonderful friend Heidy Vaquerano. Thank you for all that you are, and all that you do Heidy!

Notes on ritual/spell:

Other notes/impressions:

full
moon

mugwort
cackles, screams, and orgasms
white and peach moonstone
gratitude and appreciation
cresting waves and illuminations
the ripeness of the rose before it falls off the bud
a party lasting for just the right amount of time
the surges are harnessed
our energy a vessel
a boomerang back into the celestial
the raindrops feel warm even though the sky remains dark navy
as warm as our tears
as warm as our blood
psychic dreams
and lovely schemes
draw down
full moon
full moon
shine down
on her heavy heart
on her furrowed brow
full moon remind her
to remind herself
she is her own best self always
full moon remind her
it might be time to rest
it might be time to pray and time to create
time to harvest in the easiest and most joyful ways
full moon shine down
on her biggest dreams
on her wide and ocean crested heart

OCTOBER 12th: LAST QUARTER MOON in CANCER
5:25 AM PST, 12:43 AM MOONRISE PST

Many Moons Little Deaths

by Janeen Singer of Holy Sponge!

We are made of water. The average human body is made up of 55-60% of it. As the Moon in each of hir* cycles moves the tides, effects are felt by creatures in ocean waters, species in rivers and lakes, soil that nourishes the plants and trees, and our watery human bodies. We may be feeling this even more as the Moon wanes in Cancer.

People who mxnstruate* get to experience lunar shifts in a very sensory way—through their mxnstrual flow. And while I am sharing a bit about this particular experience, it is not the whole of the Moon-water-body experience. Everyone cycles, whatever good body they inhabit. And I believe that the way a culture views mxnstruation says a lot about that culture and its people.

Something I focus on in my work with folks who bleed is shifting away from overculture's* narrative of seeing mxnstruation as a burden to creating a more Earth-based perspective which views it as an opportunity and gift. That doesn't mean you have to be a woo-woo goddess free bleeding in the forest. There are many ways to shift and queer the narrative.

We are saturated in a culture that values sterility and whiteness over connection with our bodies. Advertising pressures people who bleed to push through their periods, buy products that trash landfills, and perform at peak levels. "Fake it. Mask the pain. Hide your blood. Pop in a tampon, put it in the little plastic can and move on." I've seen terror and denial associated with anything related to death, and periods are indeed little deaths.

Shifting the narrative simply means listening to the body's needs and responding. The time of bleeding is the time to slow down/tune in. In the shedding of the endometrium, bodies let go of all the stored up feelings and debris of the past month. Sometimes that fuckin' hurts! So taking time to honor and face whatever is expanding and contracting within the body is important and an act of resisting overculture's messages. Plants are an amazing support during the pain, flow, and release.

Some ways that I practice self-care when my body is going through the Little Death:

:: C H A R T   Y O U R   C Y C L E :: If you know when your hard days are (sometimes it's not always when you are actually bleeding), you can map this with a moon calendar. If you don't mxnstruate, you might notice hormonal shifts or regular times when you need to be extra loving toward yourself. You can use a moon calendar for that as well. If you pay attention to astrology, you might discover, for example, that Full Moons in a certain sign are harder for you than a Waxing Moon and so on. For those who mxnstruate, you may find that bleeding in particular moon phases and/or particular astrological signs may feel differently.

:: J O U R N A L :: or make time to be creative.

:: C O M M U N I C A T E :: with people you live with, letting them you need solitude or extra gentle time and space so they can be sensitive to you. Knowing and stating our needs can sometimes be the missing ingredient in radical self-care.

:: R I T U A L :: Smudge your space and your room, resetting the habitat around you as your body is also resetting itself.

:: B A T H S :: Light candles, play music, add fresh or dried plants/flowers that support slowing down.

:: C R A M P   C A R E :: There are many herbs that can help offset painful cramps. Ones I work with regularly are evening primrose (oil), motherwort tincture, crampbark (as a tea), and nettles. For me, I try to back off of caffeine and sugar when I bleed because I know it exacerbates cramps. Choose foods that strengthen and nourish you.

On my last cycle, I was feeling extremely sensitive and flooded about the political environment. I wanted to call on my ancestors whose lives were taken in the Holocaust for support, so I created a ritual around connecting with their wisdom and strength. You are welcome to use this to call on known or unknown ancestors.

Build Your Ancestral Coven

You will need:

1. A plain seven-day glass candle (any color is fine and it doesn't have to be new. In fact, it's best if it has burned down a few inches already)
2. A quart size mason jar. Make sure the candle fits inside of the mason jar.
3. A match or lighter.
4. Water mixed with either some of your mxnstral blood OR spit and a few strands of your hair.

*Begin with a prayer, call, or song inviting your ancestors to visit you for this ritual and guide it. You can do this as you light your candle, envisioning them joining you with the fire that is now lit. If you have negative feelings associated with your family line, call on spirits of the dead you feel a kinship with.

*Place the candle inside of the mason jar. Now fill the space in the mason jar that surrounds the candle with the mixture of water and either your blood or other DNA (hair or spit).

*As the candle burns and the fire brings light though the water and the actual DNA you are made of, think about all the lives that came before you and the miracle it is that you are alive on the Earth at this time in the course of the planet's life.

*Express gratitude to your ancestors/spirits. Your laugh, patterns, features, and quirks are all part of your story and the stories of those who preceded you. Again, if you are struggling with your own line, reach toward a friend, animal, or hero/heroine you admire, thanking them for what they have given you.

*Ask your ancestors to reveal to you wisdom from their mistakes and successes. You can go deeper with this in trance work or prayer, and write down anything that is revealed to you. I like to imagine each ancestor supporting me with their strongest positive traits. For example, if there's an herbalist in your line, maybe she is whispering her secrets when you're ill; if there's a boxer, they are showing you moves in a battle you may have to fight, and so on...

*Close the ritual by releasing the spirits that joined you for the ritual, thanking them for their wisdom, and blow out the candle. You can dispose of the water around the candle by using it to water your plants. If you used blood, be sure to dilute it nine parts water to one part blood.

The best thing about the life-death-life cycle is that within death is compost and the fertile ground for transformation.

hir* Gender-neutral third-person singular object pronoun, coordinate with him and her.
mxnstruate* Radical form of "menstruate" used to resist, reclaim and re-invent dominant views surrounding the menstrual cycle.
overculture* The dominant culture in a society, whose mores, traditions, and customs are those normally followed in public, as opposed to a subculture. — definition from Wikipedia.

Notes on this Moon phase:

How I feel at this time:

Where I am ready to let go:

How I will do this:

What this release will mean:

Intentions for the New Moon in one week:

OCTOBER 19th: NEW MOON in LIBRA 12:12 AM PST, 6:48 AM MOONRISE PST

Separately and Together: Rituals for Peace, Exercises in Collaboration

Hey, women! ALL women! Hey, non-binary folks! Hey, witches! Yes, ALL of you! Trans, queer, Cis, straight, lesbian, asexual, fat, thin, first-generation, poor, rich, old, young, quiet, loud, artists, activists, doulas, temp workers, politicians, musicians, landscapers, retirees, the woman over there in the grocery store comparing labels, the woman over there walking her three rescue dogs in the park before work, the woman enjoying an ice cream sandwich while watching reality television, the woman who only drinks green smoothies for breakfast before 6:00 am Yoga, the woman in the parking lot with two kids in the backseat, the non-binary person in the bathtub with a favorite book, the woman who has three grandchildren that she helps watch full-time, the women runners and the women in wheelchairs and the women with no boobs and the women with one boob and if you are on crutches or if you suffer from invisible chronic pain and if you own a company with thousands of employees or if you work three jobs and are barely making ends meet or if you are on Medicaid and disability and live with four roommates and if you pray every day or never pray at all and don't believe in the God or Goddess or Spirit or if you don't fit into any of the above or more than one or if your identity changes so fast no amount of hyphens exist to describe you because you are more expansive and more brilliant than any amount of strange-looking letters strung together could ever try to describe you...

Hey, beautiful you! Yes, YOU! I need you! And you need you! And we all need one another! For far too long, all the lengths they've gone to with the sole purpose of keeping us divided have kept us apart. Our own self-hate, or our fear of the other, or the unknown, our scarcity complexes, our timidity, our fear of saying the wrong thing, or being vulnerable, has kept us from reaching out, linking arms, and joining together. And yes, of course, we are doing it. Doing the work of uniting many different experiences and viewpoints and perspectives. Doing more than we ever have, in every way. *Some of us could do better.* And some of us need a break. Have *needed* a break. This isn't meant to discourage, chastise, or use as an excuse. It is a call to invite in a greater consciousness, together.

You all are a love song to me, a most treasured poem, one that hasn't been written yet because words can't express all of your beauty, together, and separate. You are both the medium and the messenger. I need to read your words, to hear your voice, to know that even though the world right now seems to be the darkest it's been in recent memory, that you're gonna promise to somehow, some way, keep going. So that I can keep going, too. Because some days, it was only because of you: the freaks, the outcasts, the bitches, the whores, the queers, the sluts, the weirdos, the crones, the genderqueers, the poets, the doulas, the coders, the witches, the wild ones, the survivors, the kinksters, the loudmouths, the musicians, the punk singers, the warriors, the introverts, the artists, the writers, the DJs, the organizers, the activists. It was only through looking at your art, watching your speeches, reading your books, hearing your stories, having you pick up the other end of the line at midnight, it was witnessing your breathtaking magnificence, that spurred on the hope inside of me. And that hope gave me a reason to survive.

The ask at this time, this New Moon in October, a bridge month, is to come together in ritual and meditation. In support and linked invocation. There is power in numbers. There are potentially thousands of you reading these words, thousands of powerful beautiful brilliant humans. If even some of you get together tonight, Friday (which is ruled by Venus), or Saturday night with others, to visualize harmony and peace, to offer one another support and witness, the energy will ripple outward in harmonizing pink, green, orange, indigo, violet, and silver waves.

New Moons can be invocations. We can't actually see the Moon; it is a blank slate. An invitation to a new way of thinking, a different mode of life. A fresh form of inquiry, of speaking about things, of beginnings. How do you handle beginnings in your life, new phases? Is there a catch in your throat? Do you hurtle yourself into them wholeheartedly? Why? How come?

This New Moon falls in the astrological sign of Libra, while the Sun is also in Libra. Double air, double speech, double clear communication. There's the potential for bright words between the conscious and the subconscious. Libra is ruled by Venus, she who came out of the sea in a shell. A pearl come to life, perhaps. Across cultures, there are scores of similar myths of goddesses of the sea, coming out of the sea. Oshun, the Yoruba deity of the sea. Yemanjá, giver of all. Mami Wata, the ocean goddess of Ghana. Even the Greek sea god Poseidon was first the female Posidaeja in ancient Minoan culture (Barbara G. Walker, *The Woman's Dictionary of Symbols and Sacred Objects*). The symbol of Libra is that of a scale; the Sanskrit name for the sign of Libra was "Tula," which meant the Balance, and the scale of Egyptian Goddess Maat (also associated with Venus) weighed hearts in the afterworld. Other aspects that Venus rules are love, beauty, relationships and partnerships of all kinds, pleasure, earthly delights, harmony, charm, contracts, and artistic pursuits. You can work spells on your own around these subjects, as well as with others.

When I think of this harmonic energy, it makes me think of the Three of Cups card in the Tarot. This card represents the harmonic power of the joyful collective. Manifestation is at its most potent when done as a group, in the form of spiritual altruism. The figures in the Three of Cups symbolize celebration and harvesting successful outcomes together. This card is about collaboration and selfless hard work. Of course, this card, three women, evokes the Triple Goddess. It also references the three Graces, as well as the three Fates. Sometimes when this card appears, it signals a moment where those around you can help you with your destiny, with what you know you must work on growing. For Romans, a word for signs of the Goddess' blessing was "venia," the blessing of Venus—which, later on to some Catholics, meant a sin.

This leads me to apples.

Apples are ruled by Venus. In Christian mythology, they correlate to original sin: Eve and the snake and all the damage to women that came after that. But apples have also always been a symbol of deep magic. Slice an apple open and its sacred, secret sign inside appears: the pentacle. The poison apple shows up as a metaphor for the fear that mankind had of powerful, magickal women. Apples have shown up as magical arbiters across many cultures over time, from marriage ceremonies to death rituals, to feasts and divination purposes. Later this month, people across this continent will be bobbing for them. Apples and apple seeds can be used in love spells, luck spells, abundance spells, and attraction spells. From a health perspective, apples can help with many different issues: digestion, heartburn, circulation, and nerve and brain function. Among many other uses, apples can help with arthritis, and help clean tartar from the teeth (Robin Rose Bennett, *The Gift of Healing Herbs*, pg 400). These fruits are a one-stop shop for health, magic, and loaded folklore!

In October, apples are plentiful. Can you bake an apple pie or crumble to share with your group?

October New Moon Ritual: Collaboration Stationing, All of Us Venus

Suggested Affirmation: "I call in love and peace when I behave in a loving and peaceful manner. I invoke beauty and abundance through my beautiful and abundant behavior."

Decide to come together with at least two other friends.

Together, collaborate on a ritual or spell that invokes love, peace, and harmony for one another and that also invites in love, peace, and harmony across the planet. Have components of beauty, relaxation, and joy in this coming together. It could include lots of food, candles, essential oils, pedicures, and fizzy fruit drinks. It could involve yarn and pizza! Be true to the group.

Take time to share with one another what you are working on in your own life, internally or externally. Take time to listen and connect.

Call on one another for support and peace. Together, imagine and visualize this healing energy moving out of your bodies, through your city or town, your state, the country, the northern hemisphere, the whole world.

Commit to doing one thing for yourself in the next week to invoke more love, beauty, harmony, and peace for yourself. Commit to doing one thing to extend peace, beauty, love, and harmony, in the next week for your community—whether you know everyone in it or not. Listen to your friends and affirm their intentions.

For the next week, move through the world knowing you have the cosmic support of at least two other friends. Imagine you have the support of the hundreds, if not thousands, of other people who did a similar October New Moon Ritual. Can you feel it, take it inside your cells? Move it around in your heart, translate it into your heartbeat, course it through your blood, knowing it beats in others' blood as well?

Togetherness is wonderful. Sisterhood is powerful.

Happy New Moon!

What I worked on around this time:

What I commit to doing this week around that:

How will that make me feel?

How I can bring these feelings more and more into my daily life:

Any other notes:

Charmed, I'm Sure

Hocus Pocus, time to focus! The First Quarter Moon comes squeaking in on a Friday, at the end of this month, just before Halloween, Samhain, the Witches' New Year. You've seen the dark of the New Moon morph into a crescent smile. The air has gotten colder, the leaves crunchier under your feet.

Back in August, the topic of the First Quarter Moon was all about connecting the practical with the spiritual: small spells for higher vision, the spiritual meeting the practical. September's First Quarter focused on clarity and action, both magically and practically. The suggested activity for this First Quarter Moon is to create a magical charm—to create a tangible, charged collection of items that encapsulate what it is you'd like to transpire, work on, and summon forth.

The word "charm" comes from the Latin word "carmen" and means an incantation or magick spell. Across the globe cultures have utilized totems: the Venus of Willendorf was thought by some to be a fertility amulet; the Eye of Horus, or all-seeing eye, an Egyptian protection amulet; the Hamsa, a symbol of luck, good fortune, health, and protection. In current times, tattoo parlors open with specials on Friday the 13th: wards of protection one can wear permanently. At this time, you may wish to research and connect with some items from your culture's particular symbology.

Charms can act as a tangible, portable reminder of what our current intention is. We can wear a charm around our neck, in our pocket, or in our backpack: our intentions right on or next to our body, our cells reminded, energized, or amplified with it. We can work with our charms while we are at work, or during our commute. Whenever we create something—a painting, a terrarium, a cake—we are honoring, remembering, and connecting to our intention. By assembling a unique collection of meaningful and magical objects that we engage with for a period of time, we are raising our power.

You can make a charm or talisman for protection: perhaps you sew a dark-colored pouch-and fill it with black tourmaline, yarrow and rosemary, a small shield, and a poem or chant. For love, you could utilize rose petals or rose water, rose quartz, violets, pearl, and a love letter you've written to yourself. An abundance charm could have a green, gold, and/or silver theme, and contain citrine, honey calcite, coins, basil, and a check for a certain amount of money, addressed to you. As with spell work or building your altar, it could be helpful to utilize the elements with yourcharm building. Air, fire, water, and earth, as well as Spirit and center, could help inform your charm's ingredients.

You could also make a larger charm, one you hang in a corner of your room, your work space, or outside your door. There are no rules!

At this time, think of something you'd like to create a charm or spell bag around.

Set aside a concentrated time to assemble your items, draw any drawings/symbols, or write any spells or poems to put inside your bag. It is very important to spend the time to concoct your personal charm as well as assemble it: whether by sewing everything together in bag, or wrapping it with string or twine. Take that time to be focused and to infuse your actions with your intentions. Be clear about what you want, and when you would like it by.

Some witches like to cast a circle, ground, and charge their charm with the elements: pass it through a candle flame, to charge it with fire, breathe on it to charge it with air, sprinkle water on it, and salt for earth (could also touch it to your altar pentacle). You can then visualize your intentions with the charm in your hands, and then ground it to the earth. You can put the charm on your altar until the candle burns down, then wear it or put it in your pocket as you go about your day. You can utilize the charm indefinitely, or until you feel as though it's done its job, then make an offering of it as thanks.

Notes on ritual/charm:

What I am currently manifesting through action, words, thoughts:

Notes on this month:

Intentions on the next:

NOVEMBER 2017

NOVEMBER 3rd: FULL MOON
NOVEMBER 10th: LAST QUARTER
NOVEMBER 18th: NEW MOON
NOVEMBER 26th: FIRST QUARTER

Welcome to November! We are officially in the season of morning frost, the season of the underground, whispers, and dreamtime darkness. Daylight saving time begins, Persephone has settled into her half-year in the Underworld, Mother Earth is resting, and so should we. With so much of nature quiet, we can attend to ourselves: our inner work, going deeper, getting quieter, and diving below the surface into our own mysteries.

According to Georgia O'Keeffe, who was born this month, one hundred and thirty years ago: "Whether you succeed or not is irrelevant, there is no such thing. Making your unknown known is the important thing—and keeping the unknown always beyond you."

This month, ponder how you can make darkness your friend—and how valuable it truly can be. Sink into it. Let your intuition splash around in it.

Thanksgiving is this month—a time to make reparations by donating money or time to any number of ways to support Native Americans. Learn the history of the people living where you now reside. Support organizations that advocate for Native American communities. If land can "belong" to anyone, it most certainly "belonged" to the millions of Native Americans who resided on the North American continent before it was colonized. Think about, talk about, where certain traditions come from, and why we choose to still observe them once we know ugly truths behind them.

This month, the Full Snow Moon in Taurus suggests we think about abundance and our capacities to have, hold, and give away. Our Waning Moon exercise talks about boundaries. The New Moon exercise asks us to think about animals as guides, and our First Quarter Moon exercise discusses practicing active listening.

Those who run from their fears are controlled by them. This month, stop running from certain truths. Turn around and face them. Name them. Accept them. Love and honor your fears. Then, let them go into the past. Your phenomenal multitudes need to be shared. Your unique point of view is a gift to others. It's time to listen to yourself in the dark.

This month, thank yourself—for showing up during the composting, the muck, the glitter, and the neon gradient of an earlier sunset. Thank yourself for noticing, for making mistakes, for keeping on, and learning from those mistakes. For forward motion—whether down down into the depths, or breaking the surface of your own water, look upon your Snow Moon's reflection.

November Astro Roll Call
By Diego Basdeo

A brief snapshot of the stars for your monthly needs by your one and only lunar dude, Diego Basdeo. For more information on how the planets are working with the Moon go to diegobasdeo.com and check out Lunations, a Moon-focused astrological forecast.

Aries: While it might not be comfortable for you have a lot of time to sit around and do nothing, it might be useful for you to do just that this month. Sitting and thinking about what brings you security and what can ensure your future security, as well as establishing strong emotional bonds, is worth doing this month.

Taurus: Crystalize the visions you had last month. This month, you have true staying power. Love people fiercely within the boundaries of your self-love. Remember, when you let people take what you need to reserve for yourself, whether it be time, space, or needs, you make them out to be thieves.

Gemini: Things may seem a little out of control. It may be hard to get your footing, even for a sign that has wings on its feet. Go with the flow for a while, let information come and go. Release, release, release. It's good for your health. Who knows? You might find out some secrets to the universe.

Cancer: Take a headcount of your fam. Who do you call when you need help? Who's got a good morning text for you when you're under stress? Who's got your back when they come for you? How are y'all getting free together? Make sure that the way you get free isn't at anyone else's expense and vice versa.

Leo: They said what?! About who? You better keep it to yourself this month, sweet Leo. The best confidant is one who tells and listens to no tall tales. Security and secrets are big this month and your reputation and home stability are in the spotlight. It's best to keep a low profile to showcase the good friend you are.

Virgo: One of the hardest lessons for Virgo is understanding a long game. What the stars want from you this month is to be free. It's not that simple, I know, but we can "get free," which is a kind of liberating thing. By granting freedom to others to think and believe what they do, you kind of do it for yourself. Practice makes perfect. Try it on.

Libra: Practical magic. The exchange of paper for food is a sort of magic. This month, you could understand the world a little bit like this. What are the mythologies we have around value? What is inherently neutral and what values do we put on it? How can we use these nuances to complicate our tacit consent to the way things "are" to our advantage?

Scorpio: Possession makes a really great horror movie but not great relationships. Love is a compelling thing and it may come to light that the strength of your love may be dependent on how much you can claim of another person or vice versa. For your birthday, put those hands on yourself and claim all of you. That's all we can really do anyway.

Sagittarius: When it comes to knowing what your mind and body need, who is the authority in your life? Check in with your health, not the magazines or WebMD, but your body, your breath, your day to day. Let's get it straight. Then, try something a little weird. For some people, it's alternative medicine. For some, it's a strange root. Listen and respond to the body and mind this month.

Capricorn: You put in work, that's for sure, and this month we find out what you expect in return. What is the difference between work and service for you? When do you give freely and when do you need compensation? State clearly what you expect and hold that boundary. Remember that you can only control what you do and say. Give freely what you can and with all else, get paid.

Aquarius: Your home is your hearth. It is the place to soak in all that is you, to return to your core, and recharge for another day. Take it all in. Know thyself so when someone says something about you, you will be able to immediately recognize its legitimacy or falsehood.

Pisces: This is a sort of magical moment. Generally speaking, good things come to those who look out for good things. I suggest training your eye for the good things you want in your life. It's totally natural to experience disappointment in life but try and keep one eye open for the glimmer of something special. Try not to covet or control this month. The more expansive you can be, the better the outcome.

NOVEMBER 3rd: FULL MOON in TAURUS 9:23 PM PST, 6:40 PM MOONRISE PST

Our Abundance, Our Offerings

"Enough is enough." — Dori Midnight

Welcome to November! Welcome to the Full Moon! This November Full Moon falls on a Friday, ruled by Venus. Astrologically, it falls in Taurus, an earth sign which also happens to be ruled by Venus. This is a double-dose of love, a highlight on body, beauty, and harmony, on what we crave, what we need, what we value, and why. Venus also correlates to The Empress card in the Tarot: the card of the mother, the giver, the generator, the fertile, bountiful, inspirational womanifestor. She knows what she needs and gives it to herself. She's dripping with inspiration and heavy with self-confidence. The Empress asks us to bring forth what is ready to be harvested, to see it all as a gift of self-love and act accordingly. She's the Queen of the Universe, the ultimate receiver—for, in fact, she's Mother Earth! Her archetype is valuable to take on when we are lacking self-confidence, or when our self-esteem is threatened. She knows that giving is receiving, and balances both with grace and charisma.

At this time, we examine all that we have, and all that we do not. All that we want, and why. Money vs. Abundance. As I spoke about previously, I think of the King and Queen of Pentacles as an example. The King is surrounded by SO. MUCH. STUFF. And. he. LOVES. IT. He's into all of it; he loves doing the work, he loves the mansion, the car, the wine, the status and prestige. He is the ultimate material manifestor. But he can't really move. He's tied to his stuff and his title. Luckily for him, that's okay, because that is his zone of genius. But he's limited: his flexibility is hindered and he's clearly tied psychically and physically to the material world. The Queen of Pentacles resonates more with abundance. She knows she needs nature, alone time, space, health, and focus to feel her best. She has self-worth, AND she has money. What is more important to her is her ability to manifest abundance both inwardly and outwardly, as well as sustaining nourishing connections with the spiritual, intellectual, and natural world. We can utilize and work with both of these archetypes to have a life of balance between inner and outer states of wealth and abundance.

So much of what dominant culture prizes is based on numbers and objects. Yet we can enjoy so much of our lives with much less than we think we need. The definition of wealth which only means "money earned through doing jobs" is very limited. Wealth, prosperity, and abundance are all contained within. They include inspiration, health, experiences, a positive state of mind, a calm and loving heart, community, resources, connection, spirit, laughter, critical thinking, natural talents, a gentle breeze rustling your hair, authentic communication, creativity, curiosity, altruism, hugs and snuggles, nature, learning, and many other things that lie outside the scope of what money can buy. Of course there's more. Feel free to add more. Do not limit your definition of wealth to just money or income. Dollar amounts rarely equal pure talent, intrinsic value, or authenticity.

What creates wealth? Intention creates wealth. Energy creates wealth, imagination creates wealth, passion creates wealth, actions create wealth, being in alignment creates wealth. Please do not mistake money for wealth. Please do not mistake a calling, a pure spiritual talent, for a job you do to pay your bills. Some people confuse money for power, or money as freedom.

Money can be *used* for power, and *used* for freedom. But there is nothing powerful or freeing about incredibly rich people using money to exploit the Earth, to control others, and take away basic human rights. That's cowardice and fear. But see, money isn't doing that. Money isn't making these people behave in such disheartening ways. Imbalance is, fear of death is, intense greed is, and the capitalist and patriarchal systems are.

And yet, we need money. We need to make it. We need to receive it. We need to give it away. We can't be afraid of it. We deserve to have as much as we could ever possibly need, and even more.

Having lots of money is wonderful, yet it will not solve core emotional or psychological issues. Money does not solve the challenges of spiritual lack, of self-esteem, or of psychic or familial wounds. Connecting with feelings of abundance beyond income might be a healthier place to start. The easier it is to connect to what makes you *feel and act abundant*, the easier it will be to generate more of it. Abundance can generate money. But money doesn't always generate feelings of abundance. You contain all the abundance you need. You are incredibly powerful.

At this time, examine current feelings around abundance. Do you crave more time? Creativity? Better health? More connections? All of the above and more?

One way to start is by naming and identifying simple, clear personal definitions of abundance and luxury. For some, that is a day with nowhere to go and nothing to do. Trading foot rubs with a roommate or partner. A pantry full of food for the month. For others, it might be feeling needed, wanted, appreciated. Maybe it is a steamy cup of hot tea in a favorite mug under a soft blanket on a cold November night. Examine what some of these are for you. Be conscious of identifying abundance, then when you have it, bless it. When you don't have it, give it to yourself. These feelings and vibrations will expand.

At this time, think about your connection to Earth. To the soil, to growth, to the infinite resources that cover this planet. The Earth generates endless gifts, year after year, season after season. Regardless of the ongoing violent and incredibly dangerous monstrosities that mankind unloads on the earth, the crocuses still bloom after the rain, sap still flows out of the maple tree, ladybugs still continue to nestle in-between the folds of their favorite flower. Even though mankind's greed and soulless destruction seem to know no bounds with our Earth, the oak trees continue to stretch out on the wind, mockingbirds continue to speak, salamanders lay their eggs every year in the same place they were born. Nature does not ask how or why; nature does, nature is.

We invoke abundance when we treat ourselves with love and care; when we nourish our body with delicious healthy food, the proper amount of rest, and physical exercise or stretching; our mind with new and interesting material and ideas; our heart with loving and expansive relationships; our eyes with beauty; and our spirit with greater connection. We invoke abundance when we believe through our core that we are worthwhile and have infinite value exactly right here, exactly as we are, regardless of external circumstances. We invoke abundance when we give away money to those who need it more than us, when we volunteer our time and efforts to help others, and when our intrinsic gifts and talents are in service to Spirit and to the greater planet. We invoke abundance when we take time to do what we truly enjoy, and when we expand our capacity to receive.

How much do you think you deserve to have? What is that based on? What is the dollar amount?

Our "receiving capacity" can sometimes influence how much money we are ready to ask for and ready to receive. (Or, if our money situation is all good, this can reflect the amount of love we can accept, the level of career or creativity allowed in, or satisfaction or happiness in our lives.) We have to do work around this to widen it every so often. We can do so incrementally and energetically. Sit quietly and close your eyes. Think about how much you currently make (or the amount of love you let in, etc.). Think of a number you would ideally like to make, or another scenario that correlates to your particular abundance wishes. Note what happens in your body or mind as soon as that number comes in. If it is fear, contraction, or if the amount does not seem fathomable, lower the number. Lower this until it feels like an amount your body and mind can believe in. Connect your energy with that number, and practice saying: "I am currently in alignment with my capacity to make or attract (this exact desired amount or other desire)."

One of my favorite things to do around a Taurus Moon is to build an altar to abundance. Add items that resonate with having "enough" on an inner or outer level. This can be all that you currently have, bolstering gratitude. This can also be all that you are looking forward to receiving in the next six months. These objects could be fruit, food, water, money, checks written out to a certain amount, flowers, herbs, pictures of loved ones, pictures of nature, creative resources, spiritual resources, items that reflect having enough time, space, energy, love. This could also double as a gratitude altar to Mother Earth, who has slid into her period of slumber here in the Northern Hemisphere. Gaia needs her beauty rest, and we can thank her for all her gorgeous hard work this year and allow her to be still, quiet, and wish her sweet and nourishing dreams. We can promise to give her more devotion this year. We can examine what we can do for her to keep her safer, less harmed.

You can sit at your altar every day—around this Full Moon time, from three days before to three days after—and light your candle, feel your breath, and examine what it is you need exactly. For your body, mind, spirit. For your practice, your loved ones, the Earth. Where do you need to widen your abundance capacity?

Meditate on what it feels like to have enough. To give enough. To take enough. To generate enough. To receive enough. To be enough.

Are there patterns you have around money, or other material resources?

Are there ongoing patterns you have around self-worth, or inherent, intrinsic value?

Are those two threads at all linked for you? How, and why?

What is a simple thought, action, or behavior you can work on that can progress or heal your inner or outer abundance?

Simple Money Magic Womanifestation Spell

Suggested Affirmation: "My abundance comes from inside of me. I have enough, I offer enough, I am enough."

Suggested Materials: White paper, red pen, green or gold candle (not in a votive, so you can carve) an athame, pin or other sharp utensil, three dimes
Suggested Crystals: Pyrite, malachite, honey calcite, silver, crocodile jasper, copper
Suggested Herbs: Basil, frankincense, High John the Conquerer root

Set your altar up so your crystals, dimes, and herbs surround your candle.
Think about what you wish to manifest. Get incredibly specific, and only pick one thing. If this is a dollar amount, be specific.
Write it down on your piece of paper, adding "this or better."

Cast your circle, and initiate any specific rituals that you usually do to ground your spell and raise your power.

While in altered state, dress and carve your candle with your intended desire.
Write it down three times on the candle. Light the candle and chant your spell, or read aloud your desire, three times. Then put the paper into the flame.

Put the dimes in your hands to charge.
Visualize the intended outcome. Bring this energy into your body.
Put the dimes back on your altar.

Burn the candle for three days while you are home (never leave a candle burning unattended). You may wish to meditate or visualize for a period of time in front of the candle.

Spend or give away the dimes in a way that feels meaningful to you. Promise the universe/ Spirit/the goddess/yourself that you will commit to doing the work you need to do to manifest your desire, and will listen to any and all messages you will be receiving in the coming weeks and months. Blessed be!

Notes on Ritual:

NOVEMBER 10th: LAST QUARTER MOON in LEO 12:37 PM PST, 11:42 PM MOONRISE PST

Saying No to Let in Yes

"No is a complete sentence." — Oprah

The Last Quarter Moon this November falls on a Friday, the 10th. It might appear hanging in the sky during daylight—as the Moon wanes, it rises a little later, it looks a little thinner. In a few days it will slide into the Balsamic, or Waning phase, but for now, only half of it appears, looking as if there might be a bite taken out of it: it is suspended in the half-glare of the reflected light of the Sun. In one week, we have a New Moon, another chance to reset.

Here in the suspension of the Last Quarter, let's revise, recalibrate. You may feel vaguely stagnant or discontent, restless or impatient. Maybe you want to work with the messages that came through during the Full Moon last week. Listen to the urges that resonate. During this soon-to-be Waning Moon time, examine what you have to practice saying "no" to in order to let in more "YES," a yes that feels affirmative and exciting, a yes that is a manifestation.

When we move to a new level of vibration, of responding verse reacting, of behavior, when we begin manifesting beyond where we have been, we are residing in a truly a different zone. It requires a different form of energy. We can't take everything with us. We have to let go.

We have to say "no" to let the "yes" in. It is part of the cycle. Piling one thing on top of another thing on top of another thing just will not work. When manifesting true change, we have to say no to the old ingrained behaviors. Sometimes, we actually have to reject more stuff.

There was a point in my life when I was trying to make a certain amount of money, which required people to pay me a specific hourly or project rate. The thing was, I wasn't making that much money at the time: I was looking for work. I did not have six months of savings to pad my mindset and energy tweak. My practical mind told me to take every job offered to me—I had bills and rent to pay, after all. I had to go deep into inquiry with my own scarcity mind-set. If I rejected someone offering me a job, someone who wanted to pay me money for work, wasn't I rejecting ALL work opportunities?!? No, I wasn't rejecting ALL work opportunities. I was rejecting work that was not the right fit for me in order to open up space for the work that was closer to my desired rate. I had to tweak my vibration and mindset, get clearer on what exactly I wanted. Through the unknown, the limbo period, I was to remain expanded and calm, state as much as possible what I wanted, and embrace and affirm what was on its way to me. This meant staying in the void in a state of positive inquiry, trying to remain open, tending to faith and belief while having no inkling of the outcome. This meant continuing to politely reject offers that were much too low. This process took a couple of years, and is one I still consciously work on.

Saying no is clearing out what we no longer need. Refusing to get distracted. There is an unfinished sentence. Empty space. An echoey room. For some, this is the definition of terror. For some, being in this place feels excruciating. There is nothing to cling to. No one is looking at us or giving us attention. Our ego is screaming. It wants us to control, to cling, to go back into old, yet familiar territory. Our ego wants to manufacture problem after problem, the ego creates limit after limit, seemingly without end. It wants to feel safe and it wants to feel fed, or distracted, or made right.

Existing in cleared space, uncertainty, unknown, is a process that must experienced in order to start a new cycle. Farmers weed before planting their harvest. The soil is dormant. The phone doesn't ring. It might feel daunting, but there's so much possibility! You can always ask yourself—whether in self-imposed moments of clearing or actual lulls—what needs to get worked on? What must I say "no" to? What must be tended to? On what part within myself do I focus?

I'm not saying to go into debt and bounce your rent check in order to manifest. However, if you are working towards a major shift, you must take inventory of your behaviors, your emotions, your patterns, and what needs to be moved around. At the very least, note where to withdraw your energy, then do it. Sometimes this is energetic, and sometimes this is literal.

What are you currently accepting in your life as status quo?

What are the self-imposed limits that you must reject?

What would lie on the other side of that wall?

During this time, you can throw away things, mend items, try to pay attention to prideful, selfish or defensive behavior, self-defeating thought patterns, and wrap up certain projects—particularly those that have been dragging on, Silly Putty style.

During this Last Quarter Moon, try practicing vocalizing your boundaries. Practice saying no. If you are femme, if you're a woman, this could be more difficult. If you have been raised to play by the rules, not take up space, play the game, you are used to saying "yes". Sure, of course, no problem. Be polite. Smile with gritted teeth. Don't rock the boat. Let others cut in line, steal your idea. When it is important, when it is harmful behavior, when it is our boundaries, we can say "no". We are allowed to. We can stand our ground. We can speak up for ourselves. We can call bullshit if that's what it is. This isn't easy. Usually, at first it feels uncomfortable. Sometimes, people will try to shame us. That's not on us; it's on them. It is their fears and anxieties they are projecting. This may not make us popular or have an immediate reward. But in time, you'll attract different situations, energies and people who wish to support you just as you are: a fierce lioness or a friendly fortress. Like attracts like.

At the very least, we can watch over and practice using our boundaries as well as honor our decisions to attend to our needs.

If we are to let in the yes, sometimes we must first say no.

Suggested crystals that are good for boundaries: obsidian, amethyst, malachite, tourmaline, kyanite

Where is my ego blocking me?

Where is pride or stubbornness getting in the way of release?

What old stories or narratives do I need to reframe?

What must I clear out to begin a new cycle?

Intentions for this time:

Actions for this time:

Other notes:

dark moon
and balsamic moon

when your rage has softened into grief
and your grief has melted into compassion
the compassion becomes a puddle
dark green and navy and obsidian
the puddle is big enough to swim in
but is really just an oasis for a moment
the moment that made you reconnect with the truth
the truth that fuels your power
as you reconnect to this and your claws grow back
a song begins that the crone knows
the song you too can sing
and somehow remember though you've never heard it
the instruments are:
death
gongs and panther whiskers
whale ear bones
pink yarrow and tourmeline
kyanite and datura.
towers collapsing
underneath a shining ink canvas of night lights
Kali tells you to destroy that which is destroying you
so that you may birth new facets and portals
Kuan Yin reminds you to remain in mercifulness
so as not to get swept away
and you do remain careful, in soft and hard truths
the webs that get woven
are gossamer steel
anointed by a labrys, fire and ice quartz
tears
gleeful laughter
and the hounds of hell
because you've been through it
because you've surrendered
this remains your protection
the void your connection

NOVEMBER 18th: NEW MOON in SCORPIO
3:42 AM PST, 6:29 PM MOONRISE PST

Working with Animal Medicine for the New Moon
by M. Luxe Rhysing

Suggested Affirmation: "I will utilize this New Moon energy to release that which no longer serves me, and to re-connect and establish a relationship to that which helps me to be my most Genuine Self."

The New Moon is a time of awakening, sowing seeds, and beginning a new relationship with our sacred self or that which we are currently seeking. We are working mostly with our instincts at this time, as there is very little moonlight to illuminate our path as we are coming out of a Waning and Dark Moon phase. Moon in Scorpio is a time of heightened sensitivities and as such, we may experience a new opening for information to flow to us and through us. This is a beautiful and refreshing time! We are living in an era where the "dinosaurs" of recent generations are dying off: patriarchal ideologies, our oppressors, dogmas, and ideas that no longer serve us collectively. These dinosaurs are going out kicking and screaming, and as a collective consciousness we are exposing these toxic patterns and cleaning out old debris. This is highly activated during this New Moon in Scorpio. We, too, can personally work with this Moon to cleanse ourselves of anything that is no longer helping us on our path, start fresh and clean, and begin again. Scorpio is a watery and emotional sign. This can be an excellent time to balance things out if you feel overly emotional by utilizing fire elements, or connecting with Earth to ground during this sensitive phase. For me, connection to the magic and medicine of an animal spirit or ally is a lovely way to do this. For those working magical paths, connecting or reconnecting with animals can also be a great way to go back to our roots as human animals and establish a better working relationship with our planet.

Animals are connected intimately with the Earth, her cycles, and her Moon. Did you know that birds are more active during the Full Moon? Many animals rely on the Moon's light to hunt: Coyote is a great example. Animals' bodies are made up of water in varying degrees and are subject to the pull of the Moon just as we human animals are. Many animals change their mating patterns during the New Moon, some corals time their egg and sperm release around the Full Moon, scorpions are most active in the New Moon. Dogs and cats often behave more precariously during the Full Moon and injuries of these animals increase by about 25%! And think about the animals that live in the ocean—their lives are intimately connected with and affected by the phases of the Moon.

Connecting with animals in a positive and healthy way helps the Earth to feel nurtured by her human spirit occupants. Animals are used and abused in so many ways in our world, for food, clothing, cosmetic testing, trophy hunting, poaching...We can do this work to re-establish relationships and positive interactions with our animal friends and thus become more connected to the magic of our beautiful planet.

Simple day-to-day ways to connect with animal medicine: Take a quiet nature walk and pay close attention to signs and sounds of animals, read about the medicine of any notable encounters you may have. Wear an animal talisman to invoke the medicine of that animal. Imitate the movements of an animal in dance or ritual. Help animals! Plant trees and gardens (for habitats), learn as much as you can about nature, pick up litter, don't buy products made with animal testing, support organizations that help the environment, actively avoid animal products made in unethical ways. Create animal symbols to carve into candles and to use as sigils. Build an altar to an Animal Spirit, make offerings, meditate, invoke her power. Develop a deeper relationship with an animal companion or familiar that you live with. Use an animal oracle deck to develop a working divination relationship with animals and their magic.

To find a New Moon Animal Spirit or Animal Guide, we can sit in meditation with this intention. You can read through the following meditation a couple times and then cast your circle or set up your sacred space, close your eyes, and in your mind's eye, walk yourself through visualizing the meditation. I often find it easier to record myself reading the meditation aloud and then play it back to myself in ritual. This allows me to be able to go deeper in meditation. Do what works best for you.

New Moon Ritual

Set up your sacred space as you like best: cleanse the room with sage or Palo Santo, light your altar candle, grab a stone or crystal to facilitate your meditation. Find a comfortable space to sit, either on a meditation pillow, in a chair, or lying down (so long as this won't cause you to fall asleep!).

Animal Spirit Meditation: Close your eyes and take three deep, slow breaths. Begin your journey on a footpath in a meadow leading into a forest. See the path ahead of you gently moving toward the tree line edge. Look up, view the sliver of the New Moon, and feel comforted by her light being just enough to see your way. Begin walking along the path which has been walked many times before you by many people. Feel the warmth of the air around you and continue to walk feeling secure and cared for. Follow the path until you reach the edge of the forest and pause. As you look in, you remember hearing stories of this old growth forest. People enter and often have encounters with animal friends who become guides. People come here to be purified and renewed. You can see into the forest with the New Moon glow, and it already feels like home. Enter and look around you. The woods are quiet and peaceful with no signs of wildlife. Smell the pine, earth, and dampness. The path continues in front of you through the trees, walk along the path and feel the soothing energy of the forest. In the distance, you see a clearing coming into view. Move toward the clearing. Follow the path out of the forest and stand at the clearing's edge. You see a large circle clearing with a small pond at its center. Look up and see the expansive sky with the sliver of the New Moon smiling down at you. Walk over to the pond and take a seat next to it. Pause and enjoy the beauty and comfort of this magical space. (Pause.)

As you sit, you begin to realize you are not alone. You feel a comforting energy nearby. Look around and see what animal is making itself known to you. (Pause.)

Meet the gentle eyes of your animal guide. Your guide instructs you to tell it any old patterns, self-judgments, and situations that you would like to be rid of today. Take a moment and tell your guide what those things are. (Long pause.)

Your guide listens intently and moves toward you with kindness. Then, you watch, amazed, as your guide begins to clean you, starting with your toes. It cleans your physical body as well as your spirit. Close your eyes. Moving slowly from your toes to your calves, cleaning and purifying, your guide cleans around your knees, up your thighs, your hips, abdomen, chest, shoulders, and down your back. You begin to feel lighter. Your guide moves to your arms and cleans each with care. Then moving toward your face, your guide gently cleans your neck, face, and hair. As it finishes, you notice there has been a weight lifted. You feel calm, soothed, and you have a lightness about you. You feel refreshed and renewed, and filled with gratitude. Open your eyes and look at your animal guide.

Thank it, and give it an offering of gratitude if you have one with you. (Pause.)

Your guide thanks you and lets you know that it will be here for you any time you need to be purified or renewed. You can come back to this place and be cleansed again. Thank your guide, and set your gaze back to the path leading out of the clearing. At your own pace, walk the path back through the woods, and back to the place where your journey began with the New Moon looking down upon you.

Take a few deep breaths. Begin to wiggle your fingers and toes. Bring movement back into your body. When you are ready, slowly open your eyes, feeling refreshed and renewed.

Journal any thoughts, ideas, and feelings that come up for you before closing your circle.

Other Animals Associated with the New Moon:
Crow and Raven
Rabbit
Panther (also Dark Moon)
Deer
Vulture
Robin
Snake
Bear (also Waxing)
Scorpion

Notes on ritual:

Intentions for this New Moon:

Strengthening Our Sensitivity: Practicing Active Listening

"For Nature who has all the time in the world on her side, if countered instead of courted, always contains something friendly, invisible, unknown, and dangerous that can at her whim utterly alter whatever we humans think is firm and here to stay. But we people, instead of understanding this and loving Nature for it, hate Nature and try to dupe Nature, disregard Nature or harness Nature to do our whim. ... we are afraid to listen, and continue to destroy what we should be listening to so we don't have to 'hear' about our own smallness in the scheme of things."
— Martín Prechtel, *The Smell of Rain on Dust: Grief and Praise*

On Sunday, November 26th, we notice the First Quarter Moon. We are one week to the Full Moon. I think of this time as the gentle alarm clock. If I have been sleeping in one area or pursuit, well, it is time to get cracking! The seeds we've planted on the New Moon are ready to burst through the surface, and it is up to us to help nurture them via work and effort. It is a push to get going, to move forward on certain tasks, and work more diligently a bit longer. Growing and building spells are favored at this time; it is a great time to start a new habit, particularly around health. Haircuts at this time grow back more quickly. I'm also conscious of energy inside me and around me. The energy during the Waxing Moon time, leading up to the Full Moon, can feel supercharged and frenetic. Depending on other internal and external factors, this time can feel a bit loopy or weepy. Sometimes this energy crests and peaks into the Full Moon period, crashing into a flood of waves. Usually, the Waxing time is a time of positive heightened energy, stamina, and awareness.

In the sky, the half Moon rises around noon and sets around midnight. For those of us who pay attention, a daytime Moon is a welcome sight. This First Quarter Moon begins in the astrological sign of Pisces, in the element of Water. Pisceans are characterized as highly intuitive and sensitive. We might be feeling quieter and more internal. The darkness invites us to explore within and listen to our intuition, to spend time with our quieter voices so that they might guide us. Find the subtle strength in our sensitivity.

One way to grow our intuitive abilities is through active listening. One of my favorite clients recounted to me something discussed at one of his therapy groups: "Listening is not just waiting for the other person to finishing talking!" Indeed. We witness so many people in the media, on the news who do not spend as much time listening as they do talking. We see so many defensive reactions from so many people with so much to prove, bullhorn style. If people took more time to listen, to pause before responding, to question, to try to understand one another, many conflicts would be avoided and much time would be saved. Active listening requires attention, immersion, connection. Active listening means taking more time. Speaking less, receiving more.

You could start with your body. Ask, what part of my body is talking to me? What does that feel like? If that part could speak, what would that sound like?

You could focus on your heart. Put your hand over your heart. Listen to it beating for ten seconds or more. What is the sensation there? What does it remind you of?

You could focus on your breath. Close your eyes and focus in on your breath. Where does it feel like it is coming from? Where is it flowing? Can you take deeper breaths, that fill your whole body up? Sitting with your breath, do any emotions or thoughts come up? Do certain ones reverberate and resonate?

You could focus on your third eye or inner vision. Lay down and close your eyes. Place Herkimer diamond, celestite, or spirit quartz on your forehead. Relax your body and take many long, deep breaths. Note any images, messages, or sensations that come through.

You could focus on your dreams. Rub mugwort oil into your temples and wrists before bed. Slide some fresh lavender and moonstone under your pillow and ask your subconscious or spirit to give you information while you sleep.

Extend this to other people. Try it with someone you love. When they speak, don't answer immediately; take a second or two. Think about their words consciously. Then think about your reply consciously. If you don't quite understand something they've said, ask a question. Keep asking until you fully understand what it is they are trying to communicate.

Try this with someone you don't really agree with much or do not like very much. Try to suspend judgment while they talk. Listen to the words they are saying. Can you relate in some way?

Active listening doesn't only include spoken language. We can read energy, body language and eye contact, sensations. Next time you are at the store or out in public, make a note to observe other people. Try to suspend any judgement and attempt to listen to what their spirit or posture communicates. Send them a flash of love and continue on your way.

You could practice active listening with a partner or dear friend. Sit down together. Make the pact that you will not speak. Take a few moments to breathe and look into one another's eyes. Try to express a thought or feeling without speaking. How will you do that? Ask your partner to interpret your communication. Then switch. Try this a few times.

Active listening can extend to animals and plants. Anyone with a pet knows the myriad amount of ways that animals communicate with us with no verbal or written language. Anyone who spends time out in nature understands the indescribable vastness of nature's communication. The next time you are out walking outside, pay attention to any trees you see. If they could speak, what would they say? If they could feel, how would that emotion translate?

This can also extend to environments. Different environments feel different, due to subtle energy fields: the elements, the amount of electricity running, and how many people (or ghosts) pass through can all affect the feeling of a space. This week, turn your intuition dials up a notch as you go to different places. Are some places a better "feel"? Why is that?

Our sensitivities are our strengths. We can tune in and receive more insights and information. During this time, practice listening more. Being quiet more. Taking more notes. Develop more insights. Let those insights give you aid, further messages to discover, and more adventures to explore.

What part of you needs to be listened to right now?

Who are you, if you didn't have a body to describe you?

If you could rotate your eyes inside of yourself and take a look at your insides, what adjectives would you use to describe them?

Are there ways to describe your feelings and thoughts without using language?

What I am working on:

What my intentions are:

What my actions are:

Notes on this month:

Intentions for the next:

DECEMBER 2017

DECEMBER 3rd: FULL MOON
DECEMBER 9th: LAST QUARTER
DECEMBER 17th: NEW MOON
DECEMBER 26th: FIRST QUARTER

December is our last month, even though at one point it was our tenth. (*Decem* means "ten" in Latin, as the Roman calendar traditionally started in March. January and February were eventually added.)

Like last year, Mercury slips into retrograde towards the end of the month, on the 19th. This could be an excellent time for wrapping up various tasks, both mundane and meaningful, so that the very end of this December going into the New Year feels more open and cleared out, and you don't have to do too much, other than dream and scheme about next year in front a fire or burning candles.

From a magical perspective, we have to wrap up, clean, and clear in order to make space for the new. Nature abhors a vacuum, but she doesn't love clutter either! Spend a bit of time this month getting rid of items you no longer need and examining various aspects of your life that could be cleaned up or streamlined. Take a inventory. Where is it okay to let some dreams go? What are the new ones?

The majority of this month's prompts are around spell work: crafting and conceptualizing them, creating them, and suggestions on why your spells might not be working. If you have never attempted spell work, I encourage you to try this month! At the very least, experiment with your spiritual practice in new ways, in ways that deepen your relationship with your self. As the December-born artist Patti Smith said, "In art and dream may you proceed with abandon. In life may you proceed with balance and stealth."

Where in your life is surrender calling your name?
Where in your life must you take a step back and strategize a bit more?
What has this year taught you about this balance?
Where are the gaps, where are the aches, where are the holes?

How have you supported yourself and your community of loved ones this year?

Find ways to nurture and harness your light. We are, after all, smack dab in the middle of the darkest days of our year: the solstice is on December 21st. Solstice means "sun stand still." It is on this same day that Pagans celebrate Yule, the holiday that rejoices over the rebirth of the Sun.

Depression can be the normal mood of this month—with coldness, darkness, and incessant commercialism and good cheer forced upon us at this time every year. Go with how you feel. If your cup is overflowing, if you are vibrantly filled up, take some of that energy and help others who might not be as lucky. If you need a bit of help or some expressions of love and support, don't be afraid to ask those around you.

The Full Moon of this month is widely referred to as the "Cold Moon." I've also come across this Moon being called the "Oak Moon." Think of the essence of evergreen trees that stand tall through these winter months. They've been around for ages, some of them hundreds of years old—the Blue Spruce, Redwood, Douglas Fir, Pine, Holly, and the Live Oak. Some trees can live for thousands of years! Forests are networked plants, communicating with one another through roots and fungi, sending carbon dioxide back and forth to help another and the ecosystem they are a part of.

We, too, are linked, communicating life forms. No matter your spiritual affiliation, no matter what you are going through or enjoying, this month is the time to find your light in the dark, to pay attention to messages. To celebrate, and celebrate one another, as much as possible. Create your own lanterns to carry you through these days into the New Year.

December Astro Roll Call
By Diego Basdeo

A brief snapshot of the stars for your monthly needs by your one and only lunar dude, Diego Basdeo. For more information on how the planets are working with the Moon go to diegobasdeo.com and check out Lunations, a Moon-focused astrological forecast.

Aries: Life is short and we can't hope to know everything there is to know, but we can try. And while we're at it we can strive to know the most we can about what we find. This month is a fantastic month to get into the philosophy of it all. Use your faculties of logic, curiosity, and (eventually) practicality. Learning can happen everywhere. What you choose to do with knowledge is important.

Taurus: Use your brilliant mind as a resource to find opportunities to make money or stabilize your financial-material resources. While you may use some information that's come to you from behind the scenes, it's best if deals are over the table this month.

Gemini: It's all about number one and number two! Number one is you and that beautiful mind! Number two is the lucky son of a gun who gets to share it with you! This month brings some sparks in the lunations about lust for intellect and adventure. There is no singular best way to do it. Keep an open mind, like you do, and encourage your partner to do so, too.

Cancer: Deep feels for you this month, moving from a place of macro to micro. "As above so below" is the old Hermetic phrase and it's especially true with mind and body. The state of the world may have a huge impact on you. Remember kindly, the suffering must be balanced with joy. There is depth and realness in both. Respect your hurt but don't let it linger.

Leo: Your thoughts and ideas are super influenced by your social realm this month. You may grow weary of the same information being recycled over and over again. Time to use that stellar creativity and put it to use. Be mindful not to look down your nose at your friends when coming up with new ways to see things. Being a snob totally shuts down the creative process.

Virgo: Your intelligence might bring you into the public eye this month, or at least give you some recognition. The question is, can you identify yourself as someone to be recognized? How do you come to terms with such an awesome responsibility? Take this as a sign to continue to build momentum for your work and to build new skills.

Libra: This month you'll get to use your skills of judgment to bring a sense of harmony to the discourse of intellectual knowledge. Dig into a higher level of a discipline you are interested in. Remember sometimes, wisdom is not knowing all of the answers, but finding better questions.

Scorpio: You are no stranger to the natural ebb and flow of power dynamics. This month calls on you to explicitly talk about it. I'm not saying be transparent, but find a way to hold integrity by seeking the essence of the matter, and finding a way to communicate it. You may find new ways to identify truth and a fundamental part of intellectual freedom.

Sagittarius: The most important partnership in life is the one you have with yourself. You need freedom to explore uncharted territory. That territory, while it may not be altogether unfamiliar, could be parts of your identity that have yet to be discovered. We find ourselves by seeing our reflection in others. Who holds a new mirror for you?

Capricorn: The difference between truth and fact is, fact can exist without humanity and truth cannot. This month it is a part of your work to figure out which is important and when. The key here is humanity. Understand when people need your help, want your help, and ask for help. Know when and how you engage with service. Knowledge is a powerful thing and it is best received when asked for.

Aquarius: This month, it may pay off big time to take a few nights out to find new friends who are attracted to a culture of learning and open-mindedness. The stars think you might have a few ideas brewing that could use some mingling before they come to full fruition.

Pisces: I know you love a good escape and I've got one for you this month. Keep that beautiful brain active. Think things to the end of their line. Get really out there and find ways to make it who you are. Start at home. New bed sheets? New art? Who dis? Reinvent yourself. Hone your public persona. Get versatile. Get professorial. Get freaky with your smart self.

Full Moon in Gemini: Basics in Spells & Creative Spell Work

"The way to liberation lies in using and transforming the knowledge and energy bound up in every experience." — Rachel Pollack, *Seventy-Eight Degrees of Wisdom*

Magic is an art.

Magic works if you do.

Since ancient times, humankind has celebrated both the Full Moons and the New Moons magically and through ritual. If spell work is not your cup of tea, you can always come back to ritual.

While spell work almost always includes a ritual, a ritual does not always have to involve spell work. Rituals are in our culture everywhere: bat mitzvahs, weddings, quinceañeras, and funerals are some examples. They usually denote passages: the witnessing of beginnings and endings. They imply a transition. Some day-to-day rituals could include cups of tea and Tarot, cleaning your desk before you sit down to work, or taking a shower. A simple ritual could be writing down what you wish to release and burning it.

A spell involves drawing in and changing consciousness.
A spell invokes altered states and energy work.

Some spell-composing basics:
You must decide why you need to do this spell.
You must believe unequivocally in the positive outcome of this spell.
You must acknowledge your responsibility and your power.

Crafting and working a spell is not a quick fix to be swallowed like a pill; it is an on-going process that requires commitment, practice, working, and reworking. We practice magic, living magically, and spell work not only when we desperately need something. It is a process and a practice to be explored, played with, and enjoyed on a daily or weekly basis, regardless of our present situation. It is a way of life.

You are both activator and participant. You are the spell.
Not the crystal or the Tarot card or the altar cloth or the athame or the chalice or any of your tools, memorized chants, grimoires, or herbs. You are both the conduit and the conductor!

Spells can be incredibly potent and work almost unbelievably well. (Or else I wouldn't do them!)

In general, spells act as a push from behind to aid efforts already started on. In order to be effective, spell work must extend into daily, waking life—whether that means changing your reactions, speech and communication, what you watch or read, relationships, surroundings, daily habits, perspective, mindfullness, or career, some things must be changed. It is much, much easier to start very small—on something you absolutely believe you can modify, whether it is a five-minute meditation practice, or sitting daily at your altar, or not texting that person, or being sure to drink enough water. Whatever it is, that's where you start. Small things add up fast and have ripply results. New habits become new patterns with new energy. Anyone who has made drastic changes to their life, changes that have improved their emotional and mental health, can point to a large part of the change as carrying out habits very differently in their daily lives.

That's why it is very important to accept and reflect on where you currently are and to start from there. An artist says: "When I have my own studio I can start on that larger series I want to do. Then I'll finally be at a point where I can try to get a gallery show." Meanwhile, there's no reason why she couldn't start painting at her desk in the morning. Doing anything, in the service of your dreams, is always better than doing nothing at all.

Where are you perpetuating excuses in your life?

What is it that you must start on?

That's where another witch saying comes in: "Know Thyself." This comes from the witch's pyramid axiom, *To Know*, and corresponds with the element Air. You have to know yourself as well as one can know oneself, and accept and be attuned to both your strengths and your weaknesses. It is very important to know whether your block is fear of success or fear of failure. Both have different roots and both need to be worked with differently.

With spell work as well as manifestation, it is very important to both pin down the underlying fears and feelings and to know where to be soft and gentle, and where to act more matter of factly. Sometimes, if a block is particularly deep-rooted, we know it is one that will come up again and again—so we know there will be chances, again and again, to work through the issue. Maybe one of your core issues is abandonment. This results in relationships where you hold people at arm's length. Maybe you are the first to go when things get intimate. Maybe you are so afraid of abandoning situations in your life that you hang on, for dear life, way past expiration dates. So once you get clear on that being one of your core issues, the good news is, there will be plenty of chances in your life to explore and work through this! Aren't you lucky?! And if you consciously, slowly, and gently, view, react, and behave to that issue differently, the issue will, over time, change, dissipate, and have less of an iron grip over your life. It just makes way for different issues to surface. Issues will never go away. We are all diamond onions with no end to our rainbow colored layers. Your issues can't be another reason to beat yourself up. They are the thing for you to work through, consciously, subconsciously, with action, communication, clarity, and, if you feel so inclined, with magic.

It is also very important to know and conjure up how you wish to feel, emotionally, and on a cellular level, as a result of a spell. Once you can access that place easily and clearly during spell work, it is also your responsibility to invoke this feeling in your day-to-day life. When it feels easy, invoke that feeling, whether it be calmness, love, excitement, contentedness, peace, or abundance. When it feels difficult, invoke that feeling, too. When a hardship comes up, whether that hardship be a bill, a family crisis, or the loss of income, practice remaining in that feeling, in tandem with naming, processing, and releasing your feelings of worry, anxiety, and fear.

Surprise! Sometimes that both solves the problem of lack that made you work a spell, as well as raises your vibration so that you become one with that which you wish to be in alignment with.

For some this is easier than others. We are faking it until we are making it, after all. Some of us have to find personal ways to release fear-based or trauma-induced energy as well as summon up a different kind—through dancing, through singing, or through exercise. This is what we call "changing consciousness at will" and this is what defines a magical (or creative) person. To be very clear: if you are a person who suffers from mental illness, who has dealt with abuse, trauma, addiction, severe poverty, severe health issues etc., I know that just invoking positivity could sound condescending or easy breezy. (Trust me, as someone who has been there!) The responsibility first, then, is to seek help for those issues. There is no shame in asking for help, getting on medication, using therapy and different modalities such as acupuncture or naturopathy, and doing self-help work around mental health, physical health, chronic health issues, and/or PTSD.

All that being said, here are some some spell work framework and planning suggestions:

Clarify the intention. It is better to be clear and work on one thing at a time.
Be mentally and emotionally prepared for change, and to receive messages and situations to act on following your spell work. I always tell clients who begin manifestation work and spell work that if it appears as though your world is falling apart, in the form of a breakup or job loss, congratulations! Things are moving, which is an amazing sign. The trick is to keep moving and not fall back on old patterns—you know, the ones you were trying to break through in the first place.

Be clear about the timing expectation of the spell. Do you want change to occur in one month's time? In six months? Be real with yourself: pick a time frame that is reasonable. In general, we can begin to see effects of spell work anywhere from a couple of days after to a couple of weeks after, even if subtle. Of course this could also take months or years to unfold.

Plan the details.
Plan what materials you might need, what environment you need to go to, and the timing of the spell. This could include what archetypes and ancestors you want to work with, what offerings you feel you must leave, and even what you want to wear.

Schedule the spell.
Timing is important. The most important aspect is your state of mind and your energy level. Attempting to do spell work when you are exhausted is not the best idea. If you intuitively know which times of the Moonth you will be more energized or inclined to do some heavy intuitive digging, then plan to do that then. There were YEARS where I only did magical work during the Waxing and Waning Moon. It was just where my focus, body, and energy levels were at. Don't work against yourself.

Take into consideration your personal themes, time of year, phase of the Moon, day of the week, astrological happenings, and when your energetic and mental space is the clearest. Think about how you will invoke each element, or if there is one element in particular that you wish to focus on. Generally speaking, depending on your practice and how much mental and physical preparation is done, a spell can last anywhere from 30 minutes to three hours. You will need uninterrupted time. If you live with a partner, I generally suggest buying them a movie ticket and dinner or telling them ahead of time what evening they need to be out of the apartment. I know mothers who plan spell work around naps and conduct spells in the bathroom (sometimes the only private place in a house with small children!). If you live with others, you might need to brainstorm and think of a quiet park to go to, an out-of-town friend whose house you could offer to house-sit, or do spell work in your back yard, if you have one, after your roommates have gone to sleep.

Know how you will guide your energy.
Be clear about how you will build energy and get into a trance state (i.e., breath work, meditation, hypnosis, drawing down the Moon, drawing in the elements, etc.), and how that energy will be released (burning, emotions, chanting, into the atmosphere, given as an offering, etc.) Also, be clear with the universe (and yourself) that you are willingly surrendering exact outcome. For people with control issues, this will be a challenge. Remember, you are co-creating with forces larger than you. What you are asking for might be delivered to you in a format you had not been anticipating. Expect an aspect of the unknown. Accept the lessons and gifts as they come.

Commit to action and change.
Lastly, be very clear with what you will change and what you will do in the world in the days following the spell. Sometimes, this is acting on a behavior or reaction pattern. Shifting fear to openness, inquiry, or love. Sometimes, this means taking a risk of some sort. Sometimes, when I know I will be working on a big project or grant, I cast a spell before I begin to both give me clarity and success with creating the work, and for the outcome of the project to have my intended effect. There are thousands of different ways to work a spell!

It is optimal to get into the habit of working spells regularly, or at least doing some form of magical practice, ideally, every day. This can be as simple as spending time at your altar, journaling, cleansing with sage, meditating with crystals, or grounding. Being present, noticing all that is around you and what you see, noticing your breath, focusing on drawing your breath in and out more slowly and fully. Calling your energy back inside your body, thanking your skin, your organs, your bones. You can also work a gratitude spell: to thank Spirit, invoke gratitude for all that you have, and to ask and pray for your blessings to continue for you, those in your life, and those across the planet.

You can have favorite types of spells. My particular favorite is tried and true candle magic. Like my favorite weathered and stained 16-year-old Tarot deck, I always know that candle magic will warrant tangible results. You can have your favorite reliable incenses, essential oils, crystals, and chants. It is also fun to mix up and experiment with different materials, practices, and processes. Explore different ways to meditate and channel. Read different books. Research the mythologies and folklore of your particular lineage and cultural background. Find practices that feel familiar, that are easy to build intimacy and belief with.

You can be creative with your spell work! Your painting practice can be a spell. You can infuse meaning and ritual into your art, your cooking, your workspace, your living room, your business, your exercise routine, the way you communicate, your self-care and grooming habits!

Spell work and magical activities ideally feel intuitive, easy, and like a party for your soul. Even if the spell feels somber, laden with grief, or difficult because it involves letting go and saying goodbye, it also will always feel necessary.

Sometimes, circumstances call for course corrections and detours. A sudden bill changes things, illness strikes unexpectedly. You can rework or change the intent and wording of your spell based on the phase of the Moon. Let's say you get an infection during the time of the Waxing Moon, a time typically reserved for building, expansiveness, and growing. Work to draw health rather than banish illness. If an emergency situation calls for a heavy prosperity spell during the time of the Waning Moon, a time typically reserved for letting go, work towards banishing poverty or debt, scarcity mindset and self-defeating behaviors. Then, at the New Moon, invite in abundance mentality and new moneymaking opportunities. As you can see in these situations, the immediate need is accomplished by working within flow. In this way, you utilize the energies from the current moon cycle (either drawing or banishing) to ultimately realize your goal.

Lastly, after all this spell talk, the emphasis must be on living—on doing, and experiences. On creating and crafting your life as you wish and as you choose. To quote one of my very favorite authors, teachers, and herbalists, Robin Rose Bennett, "Always remember that life isn't about practicing magic; practicing magic is about living."

At this time, our one December Super Moon— sometimes called the Cold Moon, the Long Night's Moon, or the Oak Moon— that goes Full on the 3rd, and falls on a Sunday in the sign of Gemini, with our Sun in Sagittarius, in the last month of our calendar year. Reflect on where you are, what you are feeling, and what you need. How could you give that to yourself? Are there any inclinations for ritual or spell work? Or is it simply a time to take a shower or face steam, and cook some food for the start of the week? Make some notes on where you are, what that feels like, and what you'd like manifest for yourself in the next season, months, year.

Suggested Affirmation: "I am both lock and key. What I seek is also looking for me."

Where I am at:

What I feel:

Notes on spell work, ritual, or other:

What my spell/ritual was:

What tools I used:

What I wished for:

Other notes:

Spells Gone Wrong, Spells that Fall Short: Some suggestions as to why your spell did not work

The following are some suggestions to answer a question I frequently get: Why didn't my spell work? Depending on your particular situation, the reason might be different, or a combination of a few things. Obviously, these are just a few basic reasons: depending on the unique situation, there could be other matters at play.

<u>You didn't truly believe you could receive the thing/situation.</u>
Our subconscious, our deep mind, is very powerful. Think about all the actions in one day it is responsible for: tying one's shoes, operating a vehicle, brushing one's teeth. For so many of us, these are automatic actions driven by our subconscious. Spell work is as well. If the subconscious—your core self, the motivator driving your vehicle and behavior—does not believe that these results will happen as a result of your hard work and the universe's help (the "will" portion of the witch's pyramid), then how will any spells work in your favor? That's why for beginners and/or people working on developing their self-love and self-esteem, it is suggested to think about working towards 5% or 10% more than where you are at. Start with something just outside the realm of possibility. Work with this frequently, and you'll be manifesting greater and greater situations in short time. Belief must be steadfast. Self-love must be present.

<u>The spell didn't have to be a spell at all.</u>
Maybe you needed to have a hard phone call. Maybe you need to just move out, end the relationship, stop messaging someone back. Not everything needs to be a spell. Take responsibility for your words, actions, and accountability. If you can't do this, then lighting a candle won't be able to do this for you, either. You can, of course, conduct a spell to give a challenging situation or trying relationship grace, levity, and a positive outcome.

<u>It was not clear enough.</u>
It is important to be very clear in the intent or messaging of a spell. You must ask for exactly what you want, correlating first with the feeling and desire of what you want. Saying "I want love" is a little too vague. Examine why, what, and how that would make you feel. Describe in detail what that lover would see in you, what they would appreciate, what the two of you could do together. With money spells, I think it is important to be specific, down to the dollar amount. With other types of spells, it is more important to really outline and embody how the outcome of that spell would make you feel, and what else it would accomplish.

<u>Your expected outcome was too specific.</u>
This sounds counter to the above-mentioned item, but bear with me. You have to leave some form up to the universe, to chance, to Spirit. There are things beyond your knowing and beyond your control. It is much better to specify, "I'm currently manifesting a calm, affordable, quiet home with a great view and all the amenities I need, and space for a home office, where myself and my cat will be inspired and peaceful and be able to stay for many years," than say, "I need a two-bedroom apartment on Alta Vista Drive that costs $1,400 or less a month." The first request is an open call; there are many more possibilities within that ask. The second is limiting and reliant on that one specific place, or that one specific job, or that one specific partner. There are many places, many jobs, many partners, many amazing outcomes.

The spell involved others/you trying to control a situation.

Here's a basic no-brainer of spell work. Trying to make a specific person fall in love with you, trying to control a specific situation to the exact outcome you desire, trying to hex a person (not their abusive or harmful behavior): no, no, and more no. Magic is about co-creation, not control, dominance, or manipulation. Respect one another's free will; do not attempt to place your will on them. So: don't try to get back someone who has left you, don't try to make someone specific fall in love with you, don't try to interfere with or block someone else's success or happiness, don't try to magically manipulate a specific person to give you a specific job, don't try to enact revenge on someone via magick, even if they did something you think is terrible or reprehensible. Many witches believe in the law of three: that is, anything you do magically will come back to you three times more powerfully. Some practitioners believe in even greater amounts than three! Remember, when you do any kind of emotionally manipulative or controlling spell work, you are tied to it. You keep the original energy, in some form, that you are sending out. So stay in your zone, and be very conscious about selfish, manipulative spells. On that tip, always work towards tidying up your behavior in general. Watch your language, how you treat others, and your general motivations.

You haven't given it enough time.

In general, you should start to feel or see a shift within a couple of weeks— if not a few days, in some cases. Yet things take time. We tend to err on the side of impatience while expecting results. A web does not weave overnight; a seed does not turn into an open geranium flowering in two days. If you are trying to manifest something really large, something beyond anything you've ever conceived of before, it might take months, if not years. I've had very large manifestation goals of mine take three years. Others, I trust, will occur when the timing is right. Maybe break your bigger manifestation into smaller, easily defined steps (and spells).

The spell is working; you aren't paying attention.

Sometimes, we get really caught up with wanting results that correlate exactly with our expectation—so much that we can't see that things are changing and our spell IS working. It reminds me of all the movies where little Whoever So and So is so hung up on looking for a certain specific Someone Charming that they don't notice their perfect and caring, kind and sweet best friend is hanging out, right in front of them.

A client will say, "I wanted a NEW job, not to lose my old job!" not realizing that part of their process is to leave their current job so that they can finally begin to look for work more in line with their interests. They've known they wanted a different career for ages, but because their current job paid them well and took up a lot of time, they always found excuses not to do so. Think of the Wheel of Fortune card in the Tarot. Cycles go up and down, some feel better than others, and we must have trust that the lessons in front of us are ours to learn for a reason. In the meantime, surrender a bit. Focus on your center and the core of what you must do.

You aren't doing the work.

If your horoscope tells you that this week you will meet the person of your dreams, and you don't leave your house, what do you think will happen? Most likely, absolutely nothing. We have to do the work. As situations, events, nature, and relationships swirl all around us, change and evolution can occur at any time. We must do our inner and outer work in order to catalyze a spell.

Once, I had a client who appeared impatient with me during a flash reading I was giving her at a public fundraiser.

"What's the matter?" I asked her.

"Well, everything you are describing is exactly what is happening in my life and what is going on right NOW," she said.

"I'm glad I'm accurately describing your current situation," I replied. "What is the issue?"

She responded, "Well, I know I need to finish my book, start publicizing my projects, and socialize more. *I already know this*."

"Okay," I said. "You know this, I'm already telling you everything you know. Are you doing those things?"

She paused. "Well... no..."

Darlings: We'd ALLLL like to just light a candle, have a psychic tell us what to do and somehow make it so, and have our life work out just as planned with little to no work or effort in the material world. Magical work is work: the constant spiritual practice that involves both spell and ritual work, as well as day-to-day spiritual and mental hygiene. It also entails doing our best work, with our best intentions, taking risks, trying new things, expanding our gifts and skill sets, being consistent, disciplined, and always reaching a little bit beyond what we believe we can achieve: externally and internally. Before you cast your spell, be clear on the spell, as well as the actions you will take in the days and weeks afterward.

Remember: magick, ritual and spell work take time and inner and outer work. You are in this to practice, play, live, and learn. Mistakes are all part of the process. Keep trying different things and keep using your unique gifts and voice.

What I am ready to work on with my intentions and spell work:

What must be cleared during this time:

DECEMBER 17th: NEW MOON in SAGITTARIUS
10:31 PM PST, 6:11 AM MOONRISE PST

"Dreaming is free." —Blondie

Here we are, right into the last New Moon of the year. At the New Moon, the Moon rises in the morning. We can't see it, though. How strange: a fresh blank slate, climbing higher in the sky in the morning, yet one that is invisible to us. So much like a dream, clasped dearly inside our heart, fluttering gently like two moth wings touching together in the thin cold air of the evening.

The last time the Moon was in a "major" moon phase in Sagittarius, it was six months ago, during the Full Moon in June. Can you believe how time flies? What has transpired in your life, relative to some pulsing gaping goals, in the last six months? How far have you come? During this last Full Moon of the year, consider your accomplishments. Reflect on improvements and progress. Some of our most prized trophies must come from recognizing internal achievements.

At that time, the Strawberry Full Moon, the ask was to think about embodiment. To invite in ALL the emotions, feelings, or sensations that correlate with your goals. Terrifying and exciting. Nerve-wracking and rejuvenating. Because that's usually how it goes, this life thing. All at once, a sacrifice for a blessing, a blessing that is a sacrifice.

What has come true for you in the last six months?

What phases are ending?

Which ones are just getting started?

Our thoughts, feelings, imagination, energy levels, and communication pave the way for our reality. In general, we can almost always control these. I'm not going to get into a rant here about the shortcomings of the oft-referred to Law of Attraction (I'll save that for my next bestselling book, tentatively titled *The Shortcomings of the Much-Lauded Law of Attraction*). So I'll reiterate: in general, we can almost always control our thoughts, feelings, imagination, and communication. We cannot control what happens to us. But we can guide what is inside of us, and what is inside of us is huge, it is special, it is powerful, it is beautiful, and it wants to come out. It wants to share, to help, be of service, and of spirit.

The corresponding card to Sagittarius in the Major Arcana of the Tarot is the Temperance card, number 14. It comes just after Death, right before The Devil. What an auspicious placement to have! This placement suggests the otherworldly transitional state between loss and the underworld. An unusual alchemical angel engaged in each element, Temperance focuses intently on drawing water up against gravity between two cups. One is silver, representing the Moon and the subconscious, and one is gold, representing the Sun and the conscious. The angel's will and focus blends the two. According to the scholar Barbara Walker, *temperare* is Latin and means "to mix," and *tempor* means "a season": an inner alchemical time-period. Alchemize what needs your fire during this cold time. In the Spring tend to the blooms unfurling in front of your eyes. If something has died or gone away for you in the past Waning Moon phase, or before, what can now take its place?

Spell-wise, when the Moon is in Sagittarius this is a good time to do any work around supporting your education, travel of any kind, higher purpose, the truth, luck and fortune, friendship, and fun. The Sun rules higher consciousness and expansiveness, rebirth, growth, and positivity. Any spell work around these pursuits would be favored.

What you dream about, know you want, and wish for, already exists inside of you. *Therefore, it already exists.* With spell work and ritual we create symbols for energy to spring forth—for the universe to pick up and run with. We alchemize the internal with the external via energy, intention, and spirit. At this time, begin to begin. Don't just believe it, know it. Speak your truth. Bring forth what is already within you. Watch it take shape symbolically in front of you, signal to the universe, to the present, and the future. Show yourself you are ready. Invite the universe in to co-create with you.

Spending a Night with Our Dreams

Suggested affirmation: "I nurture my dreams so they can fly free. I love my dreams and they love me."

Suggested Tools: Many candles, any crystals you feel drawn to, any Tarot cards you feel drawn to, any other magical tools like runes, the I Ching, your cauldron, art supplies, your journal, any musical instruments you play

The suggested exercise/spell is to take concentrated, intentional time today or tonight with your dreams. Court them and impress them. Dress up for them and wear your favorite perfume. Pretend you are on a first date with an exciting sparkly dream. What would you say?

Spend the next two to six hours cozying up to any and ALL of your dreams for the upcoming year in a variety of different ways. Use your different senses; take a cue from the Temperance card and alchemize a few different experiences together. Use song, chanting, dance, or yoga. Draw a drawing of your dreams or a painting. If you embroider, knit, or do other crafts, begin work on a dream scarf or embroidery piece, or weaving. Make a playlist of your favorite hopeful songs that have to do specifically with your goals, or are about dreams, and play them. Write a love letter to your dreams. Write a speech that you would give somewhere after your dreams came true and read it out loud to an imaginary audience. Pretend Oprah or Barbara Walters is interviewing you about your dreams and talk about how you achieved your dreams and why that was important to you. Bring your dreams into the bath and pour their amazing energy all over your body in the form of water. Get sexy with your dreams: masturbate or give yourself a massage while thinking about them.

What would your dreams smell like? Do you have essential oils with that smell that you can use? What would your dreams taste like? Can you treat yourself to a meal that evokes your tastebuds?

Give the Goddess who resonates with your dreams an offering of some sort: dried fruit, nuts, jewelry, beads.

Show your dreams you are serious.
We embody our dedication.

Suggested New Moon Tarot Pull

As always, get comfortable, cozy, light a candle, put on music, practice grounding and breathing before a card pull. Use your favorite Tarot or Oracle deck.

Pick a card in your deck that most illustrates what you are currently trying to manifest.

Card 1: What is already happening in my life that can be worked on to get me closer to my dreams?

Card 2: What must I embody and step into to move forward toward my dreams? What does new fortitude look like? What does my new becoming feel like?

Card 3: What are the hidden gifts of any challenges I am facing with moving forward?

Card 4: What are some elements of the outcome of my dreams, some signals and signs, that will show up to be my north star or guide?

For the next three days, spend 5 – 30 minutes at your altar, with your charged crystals, visioning, journaling, singing about, meditating about, those dreams in front of your burning candle. When you see the slivery slice smile of crescent Moon hanging in the sky, see it as a good omen for your dreams. A cheerleader just for you, and for all the other lovely sisters, witches, women, non-binary folks, queers, weirdos, and magical creatures manifesting their dreams under the New Moon.

Keep what you do secret. Don't tell anyone what you are inviting in and invoking. Don't social media or live stream it or text it. Zip the lip. Excitement coupled with the internet can entice us to share every last thing of every last cool or photogenic thing we do. This is just for you. Keep it a secret between yourself, your soul, and spirit. You can tell everyone about it later!

Bless your dreams! Bless you! Happy New Moon!

Notes on ritual:

Notes on New Moon card pull:

DECEMBER 26th: FIRST QUARTER MOON
in ARIES 1:20 AM PST, 12:16 PM MOONRISE PST

Fortifying the Present, Flaming the Future

"Don't mistake a lightbulb for the moon, and don't believe the moon is useless unless we land on it." —Rebecca Solnit, *Hope in the Dark: Untold Histories, Wild Possibilities*

The First Quarter Moon falls on a Tuesday, just six days before the end of the year. This month, some of us have just celebrated Christmas, some of us have celebrated Yule, Hanukkah, Kwanzaa, or Festivus. All of us are most likely tired from the holidays, if not from the entire insane, ridiculous year we've all been through together. We're looking to the next. Some of us are looking towards the future's light. Some of us are trying to stay fortified in the present.

The Waxing Moon time can be a time to dig into discipline, knowing that part of what you are doing is traversing into the unknown, and that the doing of the thing should be a closed loop inside of itself, that gives sustenance and meaning— no matter if you see results in two years or twenty. Today or never. Meaning: the promise of the outcome, whether it be a smashed patriarchy, matriarchal utopia where healthcare is free and everyone is cared for, or our dream of affordable, sliding-scale healing centers for underprivileged youth on every corner, mustn't take over the present day activities. Engaging in your work, in your process, in your day, must be enough. That must feel vibrant, complete. Not every day, but most days, or a portion of most days. If they are not, you must adjust accordingly. I call spending too much time in the future "future tripping." It can feel like a balm to stay in fantasies, but too much and you are too tangled up to see the road in front of you. Worrying is future tripping, trying to control or concretely know what the future holds most certainly is.

Activists, social workers, therapists, artists of all kinds, and other helpers—those of us so open to the never-ending injustices of the world—are especially susceptible to burnout. One of those reasons is the expectation of success happening very quickly, in a certain way. It is another symptom of "if/then" thinking I've discussed so much in this book, the thinking that takes us out of our bodies, out of the present moment, and tamps down our personal power. Like magic, we can't control outcomes. But if we cast aside our predisposed expectations and pay attention, we can notice and note shifts. Rebecca Solnit discusses this extensively in her must-read book *Hope in the Dark: Untold Histories, Wild Possibilities*. She talks about the unexpected effects and reverberations of activism and art. In the book, she reminds us: "Paradise is not the place in which you arrive but the journey toward it" (80). While we are laying the bricks, toiling away ad nauseum, we must take breaks to sip tea. We must invite our friends over and ask them about the sculptures they are building, the piles of silk string they are unraveling, and discuss why this all matters. We must encourage their process, and in doing so, affirm our own.

Healing is not always quantifiable. It is not a always a picture-perfect postcard. Much of the time it feels brutal, uncomfortable, it is riddled with impatience, it emits howls and wails. You know you might be on the right path to healing if everything feels almost impossible. There seems to be no language for certain emotions that are working through your body. There are sobbing fits filled with enough tears to fill a bathtub. You can speak your authentic truth clearly, even if your voice is quivery and your heart is pounding. Every minute seems to take a decade to pass. Some of the time it feels like making a difficult choice; not one you necessarily want to, but one you must. For if you don't, the universe, or your future self, will drag you, your concrete feet digging into the ground, kicking and screaming, creating harder and harder circumstances around you until you are forced to change. The message is to soften, to snuggle back around in a spiraled seashell shape, until the noise abates and the quiet widens out into the ventricles of your heart, and the sentences of your passion ring out clear as a bell. Wipe off the layers of dust in the mirror and really accept the accurate reflection: the gorgeous, flawed human you are.

Progress does not always look like progress. It is not a straight line. It is a spiral, a circular pattern. It is our DNA lattice, our galaxy, our breath patterns. Like waves, our process surges and subsides. Like the Moon, we wax and wane, sometimes different, sometimes the same.

Because my metaphysical knowledge base is primarily the Tarot, I find myself comparing phases of the Moon to the cycles and cards. The New Moon time resonates to cards such as the Fool, the Star, the Aces, the Minor twos, and the Pages. The First Quarter through the Waxing Moon can correlate to the Minor fives and minor sixes, the Chariot, and the Knights: we assess the situation, face certain challenges, reconnect with our desires, and begin by moving forward in the material world. We make the conscious choice to keep going—in spite of, or because of, hardships and setbacks.

Knights learn by doing. They get messy. Dirty. Sweaty. Smelly. They are in their bodies. They get thrown off their horse. Knights climb back on and keep going. The trail gets lost. They have to scramble through thickets and brambles, lay face-down in the muck, and find their way to a cleansing stream, their way lit up only by the night sky, the path found by intuition and will alone. The mistakes, the breakups, the rock bottoms are all part of the process. In decks other than the Rider-Waite-Colman-Smith Knights are sometimes called Travellers, Learners, Sons, Apprentices, Amazons, and Princes. All of these archetypes are brilliant: work with whatever you feel called to embody.

In the last cycle, or year, what lessons did you have to learn through making mistakes?

What knowledge and skill sets did the bungles, the mishaps, the setbacks teach you?

Have you forgiven yourself for these, or forgiven others around you?

How will you continue to move forward with the lessons you've been given?

At this time, consider the cosmic carrot dangling above your head. The ideals you strive towards, the glimmering promise that gets you out of bed, the bar that always raises, just a little bit higher, slightly more refined, or maybe more tattered, humble, raw, each time. We will always have those cosmic carrots. We need them—we need the idea of the Moon as much as we need the Moon itself. We must also remain grounded, in our bodies, in our actions, in the world around us. We need to enjoy the present, or at the very least learning—through staying conscious, through inquiry of ourselves and those around us, through doing, through trying, through attempt.

Following are some practical ideas to try during the Waxing Moon. If one or two of these call to you, then by all means, incorporate them into your routine every day. The Waxing Moon is the opportune time to introduce new habits and embark on activities that have to do with the external world and the physical body/self.

Work on something you love every day; start work an hour earlier, or stay an hour later; announce a new project or new website to the world; apply for a new job, grant, or volunteer position; socialize more, especially with people you don't know very well, who you admire and want to forge lasting partnerships with; focus on your energy, do check-ins with your energy multiple times a day and call your energy back; start a savings account or increase the amount you contribute to your savings; tend to your beauty by getting a haircut, having a spa day, or getting a pedicure; attend to your health by adding in supplements or herbal infusions or tinctures you've been curious about, or making an appointment with an acupuncturist or massage therapist; start a movement/exercise pattern/habit; have more sex, whether alone or partnered; go someplace beautiful and new to shift your perspective. In other words, engage with the external world a bit more, particularly places that will stimulate your brain, nourish your body, and offer a different vantage point and a sense of adventure.

If you find yourself wishing to begin planning and thinking about the year ahead, now would be the time to do so. Take the time first to reflect on all that you have accomplished and all that you've done in the past year. Even if you don't feel amazing about this past year, you made it. That's a lot! You still breathed. That's around eight million breaths a year! Give yourself a pat on the back for surviving, and hopefully, thriving.

If you've written in a journal, a planner, or this workbook, that will help jostle your memory.

The following is a recipe for Fire Cider— a common, very old tradition of making a fortifying and fiery tonic to support your immune system, your hope, your sustenance, and your fire through the rest of the winter and through next year. May you and your loved ones be healthy, happy, and loved. May you have the strength to resist all that does not serve the greater collective, and the courage to work for a better future for yourself, your loved ones, for the health and happiness of all people, for all animals, for the Earth, for water, for air, for fire, for the Sun and for the Moon.

Basic Fire Cider Recipe*

You will need:
quart jar with lid
bottle of apple cider vinegar
1/4 cup grated horseradish
1/8 cup of fresh garlic
1/2 cup chopped fresh white onion
1/4 cup grated fresh ginger
zest and juice from 1 lemon
dash cayenne pepper
honey

Some people like to add one or two jalapeño peppers, chopped, and any other fresh herb, such as mustard seeds, thyme, rosemary, or turmeric root, that you feel called to add or have on hand.

1. Add all your roots/veggies/herbs except honey to the quart jar.

2. Fill your jar with apple cider vinegar. Make sure all the matter is completely covered by your vinegar, and leave at least a few inches of liquid over the veggies/roots/herb mixture. Cover it, and let it sit in the cupboard away from direct sunlight for at least one moon cycle, 4 weeks, up to 6 weeks. You may wish to visit your cider from time to time and shake it up a bit.

3. When the cider is ready, shake well. Take the herbs out of the vinegar and squeeze any liquid in them back into the jar before composting or throwing out. Strain all the rest of the roots/veggies out, and pour the liquid into a clean jar.

4. If you wish, you may add some honey to your Fire Cider. You can take a spoonful of the cider a day to keep you warm in the winter and soothe sniffles and sore throats. Add some to soup, tea, or toddies to boost your immune system and help circulation. Fire Cider will keep for a few months in a cool, dry cupboard. You can also refrigerate to extend its life.

*Adapted from a recipe I've done a few times by trial and error: exact amounts were found on the interwebs. You can also look into Fire Cider recipes by Rosemary Gladstar, and many other wonderful herbalists.

Notes on this month:

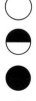

Intentions for the next:

AUGUST 2017 SIGNS: LEO : TO AUGUST 22 VIRGO : FROM AUGUST 23 GEMSTONE: PERIDOT FLOWER: GLADIOLUS

SUNDAY	MONDAY	TUESDAY	WEDNESDAY	THURSDAY	FRIDAY	SATURDAY

SUNDAY	MONDAY	TUESDAY	WEDNESDAY	THURSDAY	FRIDAY	SATURDAY

SUNDAY	MONDAY	TUESDAY	WEDNESDAY	THURSDAY	FRIDAY	SATURDAY
			○	○	○	○
◔	◑	◑	◑	◑	◑	◑
●	●	●	●	●	●	●
◕	◒	◒	◒	◒	◒	◒
		○	○	○		

SUNDAY	MONDAY	TUESDAY	WEDNESDAY	THURSDAY	FRIDAY	SATURDAY

Contributors:

Diego Basdeo is a writer and astrologer in the Bay Area. He believes fiction, memoir, and astrology have provided a space for understanding, transformation, and healing. Astrology has a particular beauty in illustrating our unique challenges, natural talents, and reminds us that we have a place in this universe as a part of the human experience and offers tools to heal present and ancestral trauma in ourselves.
You can contact him for readings and other offerings at diego.basdeo@gmail.com

Jessica Lanyadoo is an internationally respected astrologer, psychic medium, tarot reader, and lecturer. She has been consulting with clients from around the globe full-time since 1999. Her life's work is to help people help themselves through the magic and wisdom of astrology and her gifts as a psychic medium. Her style is irreverent, practical, and compassionate. Lanyadoo's horoscopes have been featured in publications as varied as On Our Backs Magazine, The Hoodwitch, Martha Stewart's Body & Soul, Glamour, and Rookie.

Schedule a private consultation, read your horoscope, and learn more about Lanyadoo's work at www.lovelanyadoo.com & follow her on IG @jessica_lanyadoo | FB = @Jessica Lanyadoo

Missy Luxe Rhysing is the owner of Ritualcravt, a small traditional witchcraft shop in Denver, Colorado. She was a tattooer for 15 years until her chihuahua familiar, Lola, whispered in her ear that it was time to do something different. She now plays with stones, plants and bones, creates jewelry from silver, and facilitates Ritualcravt as a meeting place for the Denver occult/pagan/witchcraft community. Mostly she hides out in her house collecting Victorian Mourning antiques, chihuahuas, and antique photography. www.ritualcravt.com | instagram: @ritualcravt

Adee Roberson was born in West Palm Beach, Florida, with strong familial ties to Jamaica. Her work weaves rich celestial landscapes with drum patterns, found photos, synthesizers and various percussion instruments. She has exhibited and performed her work in numerous galleries and independent venues including, Portland Institute of Contemporary Art, SomArts Cultural Center, Yerba Buena Center for the Arts, African American Cultural Center, and Art Gallery of Windsor, Ontario. She is based Los Angeles, and Oakland, CA where she co-founded Black Salt Collective.

Find her on-line: adeeroberson.com & on IG @adeeroberson.

Janeen Singer is a queer California-based business owner, spending most days in service to folks who menstruate. She started Holy Sponge! as a result of her own personal process of leaving tampons and switching to sea sponges. Her love for sponges grew in such a way that she abandoned her career in clinical therapy to work in service to offering bleeding folks new ways of seeing and caring for their beautiful bodies. Janeen is also a professional photographer, aspiring herbalist, unashamed cat-lady, troublemaker and life-long learner.

Find her on-line: holysponge.net | Instagram @holy_sponge

Esmé Weijun Wang is is the award-winning author of *The Border of Paradise: A Novel*, named one of NPR's Best Books of 2016, and is the recipient of the 2016 Graywolf Nonfiction Prize for her forthcoming essay collection, *The Collected Schizophrenias*. At The Unexpected Shape, she provides resources for ambitious people living with limitations. Find her much-loved newsletter, With Love & Squalor, as well as the complimentary Creative Legacy Check-In, at esmewang.com/e-letter.

Find her: esmewang.com | theunexpectedshape.com | Twitter: @esmewang | IG: @esmewwang

Thank you:

Thank you to the mind-blowing contributors, all of you I look up to, value, honor, and respect so much. Thank you all for saying yes enthusiastically and filling these pages with your insight.

Thank you to my incredible partner Oliver who provides me with all the love, care, support and laughter I need in order to do my work. You are the smartest, best person I know and I thank the universe every day for your presence in my life. Thank you to my special grey familiar Phaedra, you've taught me so much over the past 9 years together. Thank you to my friend Rhiannon Flowers for looking over this manuscript and enhancing it. Thank you to my friend Jenstar Brockman for deepening my awareness and practice of the Moon which led directly to this workbook. Thank you to my family and friends for always supporting me through my various endeavors and for teaching me so much. You know who you are. I love you.

Thank you to all the places that have hosted workshops and sold this publication. Thank you to all my beautiful and amazing clients who have taught me, and continue to teach me, so much.

Thank you to Sarah Lyn Rogers, the wonderful copyeditor of this book. You can hire her at sarahlynwrites@gmail.com.

A huge thank you to the generous and meticulous LinYee Yuan for going over this manuscript at the 11th hour and enhancing it. Check out LinYee's magazine at : thisismold.com.

Thank you to all my healers and teachers over the years: Shayne Case, Dawn Lianna, Emily Glasser, Ariel Gatoga, and Stephanie Azaria. Thank you to the OG witches, teachers, and mystics that opened my eyes and taught me through text: Starhawk, Laurie Cabot, Demetra George, Rachel Pollack, Mary K. Greer, Barbara Walker, Ram Dass, Angela Davis, bell hooks, Rebecca Solnit, James Baldwin, and too many more to name here. Thank you to my spirit guide Rahn, my other guides and helpers. my ancestors, especially my grandmother Eleanor.

Thank you for reading this. Sending you nothing but love and the best or better for your highest self's desires and wishes.

About the creator: Sarah Faith Gottesdiener is an artist, designer, Tarot reader and writer. Her feminist gear company is called Modern Women. She has a bachelors from Smith College and a Masters in Design from CalArts. Sarah has taught various metaphysical subjects all over the USA and Canada. She has taught visual literacy and design at institutions like CalArts, Otis, and Scripps. Her design clients include Nike, Sephora, Uniqlo, and many, many small businesses and wonderful individuals. See her design work at : sarahgottesdiener.com, her spiritual writings and images at visualmagic.info, and her store at modernwomen.bigcartel.com.

She thinks you are probably doing a great job. She wants you to keep going.

This publication was conceived as a take away for workshops I give about this subject. It is intended as a beginning guidebook for the curious human's use. It is not intended to take the place of a professional therapist or professional medical attention. If you have any questions about this work, want to book for me for design work, or wish to book me for a Tarot reading, please feel free to contact me at
modernwomenprojects@gmail.com
Love & Health, Peace & Joy and
Blessed Be.